George Watson

Watson Redivivus

Four Discourses Written between the Years 1749 and 1756

George Watson

Watson Redivivus
Four Discourses Written between the Years 1749 and 1756

ISBN/EAN: 9783337817428

Printed in Europe, USA, Canada, Australia, Japan

Cover: Foto ©Thomas Meinert / pixelio.de

More available books at **www.hansebooks.com**

Watson Redivivus.

"He being dead, yet speaketh."—Heb. xi, 4.

FOUR DISCOURSES,

WRITTEN BETWEEN THE YEARS 1740 AND 1756,

BY

THE REV. GEORGE WATSON, M.A.,

FELLOW OF UNIVERSITY COLLEGE, OXFORD;
THE TUTOR AND FRIEND OF BISHOP HORNE;

RESCUED FROM OBSCURITY

BY

JOHN MATHEW GUTCH,

A LAY MEMBER OF THE CHURCH OF ENGLAND.

JOHN HENRY AND JAMES PARKER, OXFORD,
AND 377 STRAND, LONDON.

M.DCCC.LX.

T. RICHARDS, 37, GREAT QUEEN STREET, LONDON.

THESE SERMONS

ARE RESPECTFULLY DEDICATED

TO

THE REV. F. G. PLUMPTRE, D.D.,

MASTER OF UNIVERSITY COLLEGE,—

OF WHICH COLLEGE

THE REV. GEORGE WATSON, M.A.,

WAS A FELLOW,—

AS A THANKFUL TRIBUTE

FOR THE

ASSISTANCE AND ENCOURAGEMENT

WHICH THE EDITOR HAS RECEIVED

FROM HIM

IN BRINGING THIS VOLUME

BEFORE THE PUBLIC.

PREFACE BY THE EDITOR

ON THE

DISCOVERY OF MR. WATSON'S DISCOURSES,

AND THE

REASONS FOR THEIR REPUBLICATION.

THROUGH the mercy of God I have arrived at that age which is not usually allotted to man. At this near approach to the close of life, I have observed with regret angry discussions and divisions springing up among the members of the Church to which I belong, upon its doctrines and discipline. At the same time I am rejoiced to see, there are among the more moderate members of that Church many of its ministers inculcating and inviting a closer union between themselves and the laity, as a means of mitigating such unbecoming controversies, and expressing their deep regret at the introduction of those innovations which are so nearly allied to Romish practices, and causing so much schism among Christians. That these efforts to make this union closer between the Clergy and Laity are producing their good fruits, may be seen in the liberality of the latter in the building and endowment of new district Churches, in the restoration and repair of old ones, and in the erection of parsonage houses and schools. In many parishes the Laity also are more assiduously than ever rendering assistance to the Clergy, by overlooking the schools, and aiding them in visiting and reading to their poor and afflicted brethren.

As my advanced age and other occurrences in life have prevented me from participating so largely as I could have wished in these good works, I hope I have found another method by which I may confer some good upon the Christian community,—I mean the republication of these Discourses. They have been highly eulogized by more competent judges than myself. One of them is entitled "A Seasonable Admonition to the Church of England," and, if it was applicable at the time it was preached before the members of the Oxford University, it must be considered more particularly so at the present juncture.

I will now give an account of the way in which the transcripts of these Discourses accidentally fell into my hands. I had been reading in the month of November last the Rev. William Jones's Lectures upon the Figurative Language of Scripture; in consequence of which, I sent the following inquiry to that valuable source for information upon literary subjects, the *Notes and Queries:*—

"JONES, OF NAYLAND, AND THE REV. GEORGE WATSON. —When men of such high reputation as the Rev. William Jones, of Nayland, speak in terms of commendation of any publication, we are naturally anxious to become acquainted with its contents. In the second lecture of Mr. Jones upon the Figurative Language of Scripture are the following remarks upon the outward form of worship, in which Christians are in the habit of turning to the East:—

"'Here I would observe,' he says, 'that the figures of the Scripture necessarily introduce something figurative into our worship, of which I could give several instances. The primitive Christians signified their relation to the true light, and expressed a religious regard to it, by the outward form of worshipping with their faces towards the east; because there the light arose out of darkness, and there the day of true knowledge arose, like the sun, upon such as lay buried in ignorance. To this day our Churches, especially that part which is appropriated to the most solemn act of Christian worship, is placed towards the east; our dead are buried with their faces to the east; and when we repeat the articles of our faith, we have a custom of turning ourselves to the east. The primitive Christians called their baptism their *illumination;* to denote which a light was put into the hands of the person after baptism, and they were admitted to hear the lectures of the catechists of the church, under the name of *the illuminated.* The festival of Christ's baptism was celebrated in the month of January with the ceremony of a number of lighted torches. When the converts repeated the confession of faith at their baptism, they turned themselves to the east, and to the west when they renounced the powers of darkness. In the modern Church of Rome this ceremony of worshipping to the east has been abused, and turned into an act of adoration to the altar; on account of which some Christians, who have heard of the abuse of this ceremony without knowing the use of it, have rejected that as an act of superstition, which has an edifying sense, and was practised in the days of the Apostles, before any superstition had infected the Church.'

" To this extract Mr. Jones subjoined the following note :—

"'An excellent sermon, which ought never to be forgotten, *and which I carried through the press* when I was an undergraduate at Oxford, was published on 'Christ the Light of the World,' from a verse of the nineteenth Psalm, by my admired, beloved, and lamented friend, the late Rev. *George Watson*, once a Fellow of University College, to whose early instructions and example I have been indebted in most of the labours of my life. Many extraordinary men have I seen; but for taste for classical literature and all works of genius; for a deep knowledge of the inspired writings; for readiness of speech and sweetness of elocution; for devout affection towards God; for charitable goodness of heart, and elegance of manners, I never met with any one that exceeded him.'

"After this perhaps too long preface, I would inquire if any reader of *N. & Q.* or any bookseller could furnish the above sermon of Mr. Watson at a stated price, to be addressed as below. It would be conferring a great boon in the declining years of an octogenarian.

"J. M. GUTCH."

"Worcester."

In answer to my inquiry, I did not receive any

printed copy of the Discourse, but a gentleman who is intimately acquainted with the invaluable and scarce works in the British Museum informed me, there was a sermon of Mr. Watson's there, "catalogued in a very out of the way collection," and that if I wished, he would transcribe it at a stipulated price. I did not for a moment hesitate to accede to his proposal. This was the sermon entitled "Christ the Light of the World." In a subsequent letter the same gentleman informed me, that he had discovered two more printed sermons by Mr. Watson in the British Museum, one entitled "A Seasonable Admonition to the Church of England, May 29th, 1751;" the other upon "The Doctrine of the ever Blessed Trinity." Since this communication, I have discovered in the Bodleian Library the fourth sermon, which has been called by Bishop Horne "The prevailing Intercessor."

While the first sermon was being transcribed, the following article from the pen of my friend J. H. Markland, D.C.L., of Bath, appeared in the *Notes and Queries* :—

"WATSON, HORNE, AND JONES.—(2nd S. viii, 396.)—It would be satisfactory if Mr. Gutch's Query should draw forth any sermon written by the Rev. George Watson. I never yet met with one, nor can I find mention of his name and works in any catalogue which I have consulted. Their scarcity will presently be accounted for. The sermon, of which Mr. Jones speaks in Mr. Gutch's extract, is thus alluded to by Bishop Horne, in his *Commentary on the Nineteenth Psalm* :—

"'If the reader shall have received any pleasure from perusing the comment on the foregoing Psalm, he stands indebted to a Discourse entitled 'Christ the Light of the World,' published in the year 1750, by the late Rev. Mr. George Watson (of University College), for many years the dear companion and kind director of the author's studies ; in attending to whose agreeable and instructive conversation he has often passed whole days together, and shall always have reason to number them among the best spent days of his life ; whose death he can never think of without lamenting it afresh, and to whose memory he embraces, with pleasure, this opportunity to pay the tribute of a grateful heart.'—Bishop Horne's *Works*, voL ii, p. 119.

"The same prelate has appended the following note to his own striking and beautiful sermon, 'The Prevailing Intercessor :'—

"'The plan and substance of the foregoing Discourse are taken from one published some years ago, by my late learned and valuable friend the Rev. Mr. Watson. But it always seemed to me that he had much abated the force and energy which the composition would otherwise have possessed, by introducing a secondary and subordinate subject. I was therefore tempted to work up his admirable materials afresh.'—*Works*, vol. iv, p. 370.

"An interesting sketch of Mr. Watson's character, with a high tribute to his talents, will be found in Jones's *Life of Bishop Horne*. The latter, as we have seen, was Mr. W.'s pupil, and was so delighted with his tutor that he remained an entire vacation in Oxford in order that he might prosecute his studies under one who is described as 'so complete a scholar, as great a divine, as good a man, and as polite a gentleman, as the present age can boast of."

"Jones states that Mr. Watson never published any large work, and will be known to posterity only by some occasional pieces which he printed in his lifetime. He notices a sermon preached before the University of Oxford, on the 29th May, 'A Seasonable Admonition to the Church of England,' and a fourth sermon 'On the Divine Appearance in Gen. xviii.'[1] 'This last sermon,' Jones adds, 'was furiously shot at by the bushfighters of that time in the *Monthly Review.*' To this attack Mr. Watson returned a reply, so able, in Jones's opinion, that if he wished to contrast Mr. Watson with his reviewers, he would put the letter into any reader's hand, of which he supposes '*no copies are now to be found, but in the possession of some of his surviving friends.*' Dr. Delany made honourable mention of this reply in the third volume of his work, *Revelation examined with Candour.* From the foregoing remarks it is probable that Mr. Watson may have printed his sermons and other works solely as gifts to his friends, and which may account for their rarity.[2]

"He probably induced both his young friends, Jones[3] and Horne, to adopt the opinions of Mr. Hutchinson.

---

[1] "The Burning of Sodom and Gomorrah—Abraham's Intercession." Mr. Jones has here mistaken the title of the sermon, which should have been "Aaron's Intercession and Korah's Rebellion considered," by Bishop Horne, not Mr. Watson.

[2] Since writing this article I have seen the title page to the first sermon, and as publishers are named the surmise is erroneous.

[3] Bishop Horsley, speaking of Mr. Jones says of him: "That he was a man of quick penetration, extensive learning, and the soundest piety; and he had, beyond any other man he ever knew, the talent of writing upon the deepest subjects to the plainest understanding."

"No men could have been less inclined than Hutchinson's friends to constitute themselves a *party*, 'that bad thing in itself;' and though they were spoken of with contempt and acrimony, they could have replied with Hooker, 'to your railing we say nothing, to your reasons we say what follows,' etc., etc.

"We must not take leave of Bishop Horne without adverting to one of the most exquisite works in our language, his *Commentary on the Psalms*. He had drunk deeply of that 'celestial fountain,' as the book of Psalms has been well called, and he tells us that whilst pursuing his daily task, 'food and rest were not preferred before it.' The result was the production of a work, prized by both the young and the old, described as 'a book of elegant and pathetic devotion,' but which deserves the far higher epithet of evangelical.

"Walpole, in 1753, speaks of the Hutchinsonian system as 'a delightful fantastic one,' and somewhat rashly concludes that it has superseded Methodism, quite decayed in Oxford, its cradle! 'One seldom hears anything about it, in town,' he adds; and certainly the subject was not likely to engage Walpole's attention beyond that of furnishing matter of ridicule for his pen.

"Hutchinson's own writings were given to the world in 1749—1765, in thirteen octavo volumes. Their slumber for years on book-shelves must have been deep and undisturbed. A short but masterly notice of the author will be found in Whitaker's *Richmondshire*, i, 364.

"J. H. MARKLAND."

Mr. Jones, it is well known, was not only the intimate friend of Mr. Watson, but also of Dr. Horne, and when he was elevated to the see of Norwich, he became of one of his chaplains, and, after the bishop's death, wrote that delightful volume of biography, containing an account of his studies, his opinions upon religious topics and controversies, and his private mode of life. On perusing this volume, I find the following further references to Mr. Watson, which I cannot refrain from extracting.

After some remarks upon the Hutchinsonian controversy which was then raging, and upon which Mr. Jones, and Mr. Horne, then fellow of Magdalen College, were frequently engaged, and " which kept them sometimes walking to and fro in the quadrangle till past midnight," Mr. Jones informs us, that—

"In the same college with us there lived a very extraordinary person. He was a classical scholar of the first rate from a public school, remarkable for an unusual degree of taste and judgment in poetry and oratory; his person was elegant and striking, and his countenance expressed at once both the gentleness of his temper, and the quickness of his understanding. His manner and address were those of a perfect gentleman; his common talk, though easy and fluent, had the correctness of studied composition; his benevolence was so great that all the beggars of Oxford knew the way to his chamber door; upon the whole, his character was so spotless, and his conduct so exemplary, that, mild and gentle as he was in his carriage towards them, no young man dared to be rude in his company, By many of the first people in the University he was known and admired, and it being my fortune to live in the same staircase with him, he was very kind and attentive to me, though I was much his junior; he often allowed me the pleasure of his conversation, and sometimes gave me the benefit of his advice, of which I knew the meaning to be so good, that I always heard it with respect, and followed it as well as I could. This gentleman was a Hebrew scholar, and a favourer of Mr. Hutchinson's philosophy, but had kept it to himself, in the spirit of Nicodemus, and when I asked him the reason of it afterwards, and complained of the reserve with which he had so long treated me, 'Why,' said he, 'these things are in no repute, the world does not receive them, and you being a young man who must keep what friends you have, and make your fortune in the world, I thought it better to let you go on in your own way, than bring you into that embarrassment which might be productive of more harm than good, and embitter the future course of your life; besides it is far from being clear to me how you would receive them, and then I might have lost your friendship.' It was now too late for such a remonstrance to have any effect, I therefore, on the contrary, prevailed upon him to become my master in Hebrew, which I was very desirous to learn, and in this he acquitted himself with so much skill and kind attention, writing out for me with his own hand such grammatical rules and directions as he judged necessary, that in a very short time I could go on without any guide."

"To this gentleman, whose name was Watson, I recommended Mr. Horne, at my departure from Oxford, and they were so well pleased with each other, that Mr. Horne, instead of going home to his friends in the vacation, stayed for the advantage of following his studies at Oxford under the direction of his new teacher; and in the autumn of 1749, he began a series of letters to his father, which fill above thirty pages in large quarto, very closely written, from the whole tenor of which it is pleasant to see how entire a friendship and confidence there was between a grave and learned father and a son not yet twenty years of age."

Having first apologized to his father for not visiting him in vacation, Mr. Horne gives an account of his teacher:—

"I am obliged for the happiness I have enjoyed of late to a gentleman of this society, and shall always bless God that his providence ever brought me acquainted with him. He is fellow of our house, and though but six and twenty, as complete a scholar in the whole circle of learning, as great a divine, as good a man, and as polite a gentleman as the present age can boast of."

These words of Mr. Horne I introduce with peculiar satisfaction, because they afford so strong a concurring testimony to the truth of what I have already ventured to say of Mr. Watson. His sermon on the nineteenth Psalm, which he preached before the University, and afterwards left the printing of it to his care, so delighted Mr. Horne (as it appears from letters to his father), "*that it probably raised in his mind the first desire of undertaking that Commentary on the whole Book of Psalms, which he afterwards brought to such perfection.*"—pp. 251, 28, 1st Edition, 1795.

There are other allusions to Mr. Watson in Mr. Jones's Life of the Bishop, but after extracting the foregoing high eulogiums upon his talents and character, it would be superfluous to assign any other reason for my undertaking the republication of the *Four Sermons*, transcripts of which I have been so fortunate to obtain. The remarkable difficulty in meeting with any of his publications has been suggested by Mr. Markland. But if none of them had been brought to light, the suggestion made by Mr. Jones, and perhaps with reason, that it was Mr. Watson's conversation and writings which induced the bishop to compose his valuable and popular *Commentary upon the Psalms*, is a result which must rejoice the heart of every inquirer into their beauty and excellence.

It may be asked why a layman, professing little knowledge of philology, should have undertaken this reprint of discourses, in the notes to which are so many references to the learned languages, Hebrew, Greek, and Latin? My first reason is, that the transcripts I have received are so legibly and carefully written, that I think they may safely be committed to the press, and that I have been fortunate in obtaining the revision of the proofs by a friend fully competent to the task, so that I hope few errata will be found. Secondly, I have for the last two years been living in retirement, and preparing, by a more diligent study of my Bible, Bishop Horne's Commentary, and other religious works, for that change from this world to another, which cannot be far distant. Could I flatter myself that any one would read these discourses with half the pleasure that I have done in reprinting them, he would not lament the loss of his labour. To use Bishop Horne's words—" The employment has detached me from the bustle and hurry of life, the din of politics, and the noise of folly."

The following are the subjects of the four Discourses now submitted for republication :—

1. Christ the Light of the World.
2. The Seasonable admonition to the Church of England.
3. Aaron's Intercession and Korah's Rebellion considered.
4. The Doctrine of the ever Blessed Trinity.

I may be allowed to remark that the character of these Discourses is various. That they were written by a man of quick penetration, of extensive learning, and the soundest piety. They are more argumentative than declamatory. The opinions of the writer are verified by numerous texts of Scripture, showing his intimate acquaintance with the whole of the Sacred Writings ; in style, energy, and classic elegance, they all rank amongst the best compositions ; animated with the sublimest strains of devotion, and expressing the justest notions of God's providence and attributes. When the whole of them are so excellent it may be invidious to speak of one in preference to another, but I cannot refrain from recommending to special notice the fourth, in which the author has so ably vindicated the doctrine of the ever-blessed Trinity, which may in truth be called a masterpiece of sound learning and close reasoning.

Of Mr. Watson's parentage, and the public or private school in which he was educated before he entered at University College, I regret that I have been unable hitherto to obtain any account. Dr. Hessey, the head master of Merchant Taylors' School, has informed me he cannot find his name in the registry. Upon inquiry of Dr. Kynaston, the head master of St. Paul's, he has not given me any reply.

The following extracts, from the Registers of the College, have been kindly sent me by the present master, Dr. Plumptre. The entry in the book upon his admission is as follows:—

"Ego Georgius Watson, filius unicus Humphredi Watson, Armigeri de Lond., lubens subscribo sub tutamine Magistri Nelson, annos natus sedecim, Martii 14, 1739-40."

He was elected to a scholarship on the Bennet Foundation December 13th, 1744, and to a fellowship on the same Foundation October 27th, 1747, which he resigned March 20th, 1754. Dr. Plumptre adds, that he could not find in University College Library any copies of works written by him, except two of Mr. Watson's sermons, on "Christ the Light of the World," and "Aaron's Intercession," which have since been found bound up in a volume of Miscellaneous Sermons in the Library attached to the Master's Lodgings in University College, and that he has no means of ascertaining what was his position in life after he left college.

By the above entry it appears that his father resided in London, and being designated *Armiger*, he must have been of some position in society.

Having endeavoured to discover what were the pursuits in life of Mr. Watson after he resigned his fellowship and left the university, and where he might subsequently have officiated as a minister of the gospel, the only information I have obtained was the following communication to the *Notes and Queries*, while this preface was preparing.

"REV. GEORGE WATSON (2nd S. viii, 396; ix, 281, 355). —I have only during the last few days been able to look over *N. & Q.* for the last four months.

"I have in my possession a MS. Sermon, given me by my father some years ago, and upon which, on his authority, I marked the name of Rev. George Watson as the author. I have every reason to believe in the correctness of this statement, as the subject of Mr. Gutch's inquiry was an intimate friend of my great-grandfather, the Rev. Benjamin Rudge. Had I time, I think I should find in my father's correspondence some particulars of Mr. Watson. Perhaps a search amongst the records of Winchester School might give some information.

"The text of the sermon referred to is James iv, 6, and at the end are reference to Eccles. vii, 8, Proverbs iii, 34, as if the sermon was to do duty for each of the three texts.

"The sermon has evidently been used by others besides its author.

"Whether my father had many of Mr. Watson's sermons I cannot say; if so, they were gradually destroyed. I have, however, fragments of two, which from a comparison of handwriting are, I think, by Mr. Watson, rather than by Mr. Rudge. One was intended for a sermon on Isaiah lxiii, 1. The subject of the other is the Resurrection.

"F. B. RELTON."

"Dacre Park, Lee."

On putting myself in communication with Mr. Relton, he has informed me, his avocations are such, that he cannot spare time to search into his father's papers; but he has kindly sent me the manuscript sermon which he supposes to be in the handwriting of Mr. Watson, though interpolated by Mr. Rudge. The sermon is composed very much in the style in which Mr. Watson expounded the Scriptures, but I think he had adapted it to a different class of persons than those whom he addressed in the university pulpit. As I had printed the four sermons of which I had obtained transcripts before I received Mr. Relton's manuscript, I have not thought it necessary to add it to them. The fragments of the other two manuscript sermons are compiled far more elaborately, and would, if entire, have been a valuable addition to the present series of Mr. Watson's sermons.

I cannot help again regretting Mr. Relton's inability to search his father's letters; although I am now pretty well satisfied that the remaining days of Mr. Watson's life must have been devoid of public interest. His remarks upon men and passing events must of course have been interesting, had such appeared in his letters, but his quiet college life may have presented few events, and his later days may have been passed in study and retirement.

That invaluable repertory for names and dates, the Index to the *Gentleman's Magazine,* has been searched, but no mention of the Reverend George Watson has been found.

In conclusion; I must record how much I am indebted to my friend Mr. Markland for the assistance which he has rendered me during the republication of these sermons. I have found him my energetic ally. He has afforded me his mature advice, he has written several letters for information in relation to Mr. Watson, and obtained many of those names which dignify the list of subscribers. Though he had not read the sermons himself, yet he felt so well satisfied with the testimony borne to their merits by Horne and Jones, that if I hesitated, he encouraged—if I doubted, he decided. He will therefore be pleased to accept my grateful thanks for the services which he has rendered me.

With these explanations I do not hesitate to commit these discourses to the judgment and criticism of a discerning public.

JOHN MATHEW GUTCH.

Barbourne, Worcester, Nov. 1860.

CHRIST THE LIGHT OF THE WORLD.

A

SERMON

PREACHED BEFORE THE UNIVERSITY OF OXFORD,

AT

ST. PETER'S,

ON SATURDAY, OCTOBER 28th, 1749.

BY

GEORGE WATSON, M.A.,
FELLOW OF UNIVERSITY COLLEGE.

PUBLISHED BY REQUEST.

OXFORD:

PRINTED AT THE THEATRE FOR SACKVILLE PARKER, AND SOLD BY M. COOPER, AT THE GLOBE IN PATER-NOSTER ROW, LONDON.

M.DCC.L.

Imprimatur,

J. PURNELL,

Vice-Can. Oxon.

Dec. 23, 1749.

TO THE

VICE-CHANCELLOR

AND

UNIVERSITY OF OXFORD,

PARTICULARLY THE

MASTER AND FELLOWS

OF

UNIVERSITY COLLEGE,

THIS DISCOURSE

IS

WITH ALL GRATITUDE AND RESPECT,

HUMBLY INSCRIBED

BY

THE AUTHOR.

PREFACE.

The design of this discourse is to recommend the study of the sacred scriptures to persons of true taste and genius, as books intended for our delight, as well as instruction. I have long observed with concern, that these holy pages seem to have lost much of that reverence with which they used to be received among Christians: this, I fear, is in a great measure owing to the common method of expounding them; whereby, little or no regard being had to their spiritual intention, that particular, in which they most excel all other writings whatever, becomes every day less known, and they are shamefully reduced to the low standard of human compositions. I have for this reason, in the following exposition of the xixth psalm, chiefly insisted upon the prophetical sense, taking no other notice all along of the literal and obvious one, than is absolutely requisite to the right understanding of the spiritual. It may perhaps be expected, that I should make some apology here for troubling the reader with so many quotations: I hope it will be esteemed a suf-cient one, if I say I did not add them out of ostentation; but because I thought what I had to offer would not only find a considerable support in the sanction of great and approved authorities, but be also on that account less liable to exception, at least stand free from all imputation of singularity and novelty. I am sensible I am very far from having done justice to my subject; but hope this rude and imperfect essay, if it should meet with a favourable reception, will be a means of engaging others, who are better qualified, to dedicate the great abilities God has graciously bestowed upon them, to a work so highly laudable and beneficial at all times, so particularly necessary in those wherein we live: that so the Christian world may be bettered by their labours, and men grow more and more enamoured of these holy books, whose peculiar character it is, that in them, and them alone, is contained that " excellency of knowledge," for which every one, who has with the Apostle experienced the blessedness of it, will, like him, I am certain, " count all things but loss."

CHRIST THE LIGHT OF THE WORLD.

A SERMON.

PSALM XIX, 4, 5, 6.

In them hath he set a tabernacle for the sun, which is as a bridegroom coming out of his chamber, and rejoiceth as a strong man to run a race. His going forth is from the end of the heaven, and his circuit unto the ends of it, and there is nothing hid from the heat thereof.

THE sun here spoken of, in the full and prophetical sense of the expression, is, I think, Christ, and the psalm from which the text is taken a glorious and animated description of his rising and the blessed effects of it. He is here, as in other places of holy writ, represented to our senses under the image of the material sun, doing in the spiritual or moral world what that does in the natural. This will, I hope, fully appear in the ensuing discourse, in which I shall

I. Lay before you at large my reasons for this exposition.

II. Shew the propriety of Christ's being thus represented to us.

III. Give a short paraphrase, and comment where

I think it necessary, upon the whole psalm; that the sense in which I understand it, together with the connection and beauty of this divine composition, may be seen at one view. And

IV. Conclude with an exhortation, to encourage you to do all that in you lies for the preservation and support of the great and comfortable truth, which it is the design of this discourse to establish. I am

1. To lay before you at large my reasons for this exposition. And here I shall begin with observing that Christ is the chief or principal subject of the psalms in general. "The sacred psalter," says an able Latin paraphrast in his preface to it, "is a divine and admirable instrument of the Holy Spirit, variously expounded by different hands, scarce yet understood, sometimes corrupted by hereticks; which contains in it as many mysteries as it does words, whose roots are not fixed in earth but heaven, since Christ is there, who is the substance and scope of it."[1] And, indeed, it can be looked upon as nothing less than a rich storehouse of Christian knowledge. Upon whatever occasion any

---

[1] "Psalterium sacrosanctum est divinum et admirabile spiritûs sancti organum, variè à diversis interpretatum, vixdum intellectum, nonnunquam ab hæreticis corruptum, cui tot sunt mysteria quot verba. Cujus radices non in terrâ, sed in cœlo fixæ sunt, cum ibidem sit CHRISTUS, qui ipsius materia est et intentio."—Rayner. Snoygoudani, *Med. Paraphr. in Psalm.* Lugd., 1542.

of these divine hymns were composed, the inspired author uses that only as a channel to convey some great and important truth concerning the latter times; the literal sense is only a clothing to the spiritual; the various wonders and mighty deliverances therein recorded, the sufferings and actions therein described, being all typical of far greater wonders to be accomplished, mightier deliverances to be wrought, infinitely superior sufferings to be sustained, infinitely superior actions to be performed—even the wonderful scheme of man's redemption, his deliverance from death and hell, the sufferings and actions of the Son of God: to him every page relates, has its full completion in him. It is impossible to give examples of this at present, that of itself affording sufficient matter for a whole discourse of this kind; but every reader's own observation, when he has this key given to him, may collect more than enough for his conviction.

2. S. Paul has taken the natural images in the 4th verse of this psalm, and applied them spiritually, to the manifestation of the light of life by the preaching of his apostles. The place is in the x. chapter of his epistle to the Romans, and the application as express as possible. He is speaking of those Jews who had not obeyed the gospel—"But I say," argues the Apostle, "have they not heard? Yes verily."—Then immediately follows the quotation from this psalm—"Their sound went out into all the

earth, and their words unto the ends of the world"[1]—As if he had said, they must have heard, as the Apostles were commanded not to turn unto the gentiles, till they had published their glad tidings throughout Judea; but the knowledge of him is now become universal, all flesh has seen the glory of the Lord; the light divine, like that in the heavens, has visited the whole world, as the prophet David[2] foretold in the xixth psalm. If such then was the Prophet's meaning, as is evident from the Apostle's application, if the heavens thus declare the glory of God, and this is the great lesson they are incessantly teaching; what other language do they speak, than that their Lord is the representative of ours, the bright ruler in the natural world of the more glorious one in the spiritual, their sun of the *Sun of Righteousness?*

---

[1] The Apostle cannot be supposed to have made use of this scripture in a sense of accommodation only, because he cites it among other texts, which he produces merely as prophecies.

[2] "Cujus (Christi) et prædicatores Apostolis (it should be Apostoli) in Psalmis David ostenduntur—In universâ, inquit, terrâ exiit sonus eorum, et usque ad terminos terræ verba eorum."—Tertull. *Adv. Jud.*, c. 7. Edit. Lut. Paris. 1675. He says in another place that when our Lord sent his Apostles out to preach, this scripture was fulfilled—"Siquidem et Apostolos mittens ad prædicandum universis nationibus, in omnem terram exire sonum eorum et in terminos terræ voces eorum, psalmum adimplendo, præcipit."—Id. *Adv. Marcion.*, lib. iv, ad fin. See also Just. Martyr, p. 60, edit. Lond. 1722.

3. The title of this psalm directs us to apply it to him. The title is—"For the Conqueror," not "chief Musician," the word here used having no such sense any where in scripture, but signifying only conqueror, or conquest;[1] and accordingly Pagninus[2] has so translated it. "A psalm *for* David," as the Chaldee Paraphrast,[3] the LXX,[4] and Pagninus,[5] have rightly rendered it, not "*of* David,"[6] the particle[7] prefixed to the word David manifestly making it the dative case: so that the whole title together is—"For the Conqueror, a psalm for David"—for him of whom it is said in the book of Revelations, that he went out conquering and to conquer[8]—the true David, the beloved Son of God.

---

[1] לַמְנַצֵּחַ.   [2] Victori.   [3] לְדָוִד.
[4] Τῷ Δαβίδ.   [5] Davidi.

[6] If this had been the sense of the inspired writer, the word David would, I am persuaded, have been put in regimen, as it is every where else—as in the *soul of David, men of David, enemies of David, words of David*, etc. And as this construction seems to depend on the word translated *A Psalm* being placed before *ledavid*, I would farther observe here, that it is often put after—as in Ps. xxiv, lxviii, ci, cix, cx, cxxxix, etc. And we frequently meet with *ledavid* without it; sometimes joined with other words, as in Ps. xiv, xviii, lxx, etc.; and sometimes by itself, as in Ps. xxv, xxvi, xxvii, xxviii, xxxiv, xxxv, etc. To suppose מִזְמוֹר, a psalm, to be understood in the two last-mentioned instances, and to admit it into the translation upon no better grounds than conjecture, is, I humbly think, a liberty that ought not to be taken with the sacred text.

[7] לְדָוִד.   [8] Rev. vi, 2.

4. If Christ is not the sun or light here spoken of, the former and latter part of this psalm seem not to have so exact a connection,[1] if any, with one another: for immediately upon this fine description of the light, and its extensive and beneficial progress, we read—"The law of the Lord is perfect, converting the soul, the testimony of the Lord is sure, making wise the simple," &c., where the transition does not appear to be easy and natural. But if we carry on our thoughts, as all who would understand the scriptures must, from natural to spiritual objects, taking our ideas of the latter from the former, and understand this of the true light,

---

[1] There can be no just parallel, I think, drawn between the sun and the law; since even after it went forth out of Zion (a complete and perfect dispensation, with all its types realized, and its prophecies accomplished) it never had any light of its own, shone only with the lustre it received from Christ, who is the fountain of light in the spiritual world, the father of all the lesser lights that have ever appeared, which are so called in holy writ for no other reason but because they either represented, or directed men to Him: and if, as is here supposed, it is in this sense alone that the law is ever said to enlighten, namely as it is the means of leading us to the true and only source of divine light and perfection—then is Christ, properly speaking, the light it conveys; and the comparison in this place should be made, not between the material sun, and the law, which, by images taken from him, directs men to the spiritual, but between the two principals, the material sun and the Sun of Righteousness himself.

as S. John emphatically styles him, the person the material light represents—then all is beautiful and consistent, one thought pursued throughout the whole, the design of this divine composition exactly regular, and the piece, as one may be certain every work is of which God is the author, finished and perfect to the last degree.

5. This of the sun or light is, above all others, the title by which he was always distinguished. Thus, as Justin Martyr observes, "the Holy Spirit styles him the 'Glory of the Lord.'"[1] Balaam calls him "The star that was to come out of Jacob."[2] David[3] says of him "That he should rise as the light of the morning, even a morning without clouds."[4] Isaiah is very particular—"Arise, shine, for thy light is

---

[1] Ἡ τις καὶ δόξα Κυρίου ὑπὸ Πνεύματος ἁγίου καλεῖται, ποτὲ δὲ σοφία, ποτὲ δὲ ἄγγελος, ποτὲ δὲ Θεὸς, ποτὲ δὲ κύριος, καὶ λόγος. *Dialog. cum Tryph.*, p. 266, edit. Lond. I need not multiply authorities in defence of a point so generally allowed: as a very remarkable one, however, at present occurs to me, I will set it down. Ps. lxxxv (one of the proper psalms for Christmas Day), ver. 10. *That glory may dwell in our land.* This the learned paraphrast above cited expounds in the following manner, " Ut inhabitet CHRISTUS, qui est GLORIA Patris."—*Synog.*, p. 279.

[2] Numb. xxiv, 17.   [3] 2 Sam. xxiii, 4.

[4] באור בקר יזרח שמש—The Prophet must unquestionably, I think, be supposed to speak of his rising, as it can with no propriety be said, that the natural sun should *arise as the light of the morning*, which is the literal translation of the Hebrew.

come, and the glory of the Lord is risen upon thee: for behold, darkness shall cover the earth, and gross darkness the people; but the Lord shall arise upon thee, and his glory shall be seen upon thee, and the gentiles shall come to thy light, and kings to the brightness of thy rising."[1] And again—"The sun shall be no more thy light by day, neither for brightness shall the moon give light unto thee, but the Lord shall be unto thee an everlasting light, and thy God thy glory,"[2] etc. And Malachi foretells his coming in these remarkable words—"But upon you that fear my name shall the Sun of Righteousness arise with healing in his wings."[3] Zecharias, after this, styles him "The day-spring from on high"[4]— Simeon alluding to the prophecies which thus described him, "A light to lighten the gentiles, and the glory of his people Israel"[5]— S. John—"The light that shined in darkness," that of which the Baptist was sent to bear witness, "The true light, which lighteth every man that cometh into the world."[6] And, to mention no more, he expressly affirms it of himself—"I am the light of the world; he that followeth me shall not walk in darkness, but shall have the light of life."[7]

6. For the farther confirmation of this opinion, we may observe, that the characters to which the sun is here compared are two of our blessed Lord's

---

[1] Isaiah lx, 3.   [2] Ib. 19.   [3] Mal. iv, 2.
[4] Luke i, 78.   [5] Ib. ii, 32.   [6] John i, 5, 7, 9.   [7] Ib. viii, 12.

peculiar titles—We will consider each of them separately. And

First, he is the bridegroom. He was all along promised to the Church under this title: his love to it, and mystical union with it, are throughout the sacred writings, especially in the Canticles, described by the most tender images, taken from the love and union between husband and wife. He calls himself by this name in his answer to John's disciples—" And Jesus said unto them, Can the children of the bride-chamber mourn as long as the bridegroom is with them? But the days will come, when the bridegroom shall be taken away from them, and then shall they fast."[1] To mention but two places more, he is again thus described in the triumphant song of the great multitude, recorded in the xixth chapter of the Revelations, who said " Alleluia, for the Lord God omnipotent reigneth: let us be glad, and rejoice, and give honour to him, for the marriage of the Lamb is come, and his wife hath made herself ready."[2] And in the next chapter but one, the beloved disciple tells us, " I John saw the holy city, new Jerusalem, coming down from God out of heaven, prepared as a bride adorned for her husband."[3]

Secondly, he is the strong man. He is frequently in the prophetical writings spoken of under this title. This is the word in the lxxxixth psalm,

---

[1] Matth. ix, 15.   [2] *Ib.* 6, 7.   [3] Rev. xxi, 2.

where we read, "Then thou spakest in vision to thy holy one,[1] and saidst, I have laid help upon one that is mighty, I have exalted one chosen out of the people; I have found David, my servant, with my holy oil have I anointed him."[2] Now that the person here spoken of is not to be confined to the type, or earthly David, but carried on to, and understood of that David, of whom it was foretold[3] many years after the son of Jesse was dead, that God would raise him up to be their king and shepherd —no Christian, I presume, will be inclined to dispute. And if he is the David here mentioned, so by consequence, the holy one, the chosen, the anointed, all eminently his titles—then is he also Ge Ber, or the mighty one, and this one of his titles.

Again, he is thus styled in another remarkable prophecy concerning his sufferings—"Awake, O sword, against my shepherd, and against the man that is my fellow, saith the Lord of hosts,"[4] etc., where the word in the original for man is that before-mentioned, Ge Ber, or the strong man. Now it cannot be questioned who we are to understand by "my shepherd," "the great shepherd of the sheep,"[5]

---

[1] It should be "merciful one," לַחֲסִידְךָ, "misericordi tuo."—Pagn.

[2] Ver. 19, etc.

[3] Jeremiah xxx, 9; Hos. iii, 5; Ezek. xxxiv, 23, 24; xxxvii, 24, 25, etc.

[4] Zech. xiii, 7.   [5] Heb. xiii, 20.

or "my fellow" (in the orig., *my united one*)[1], the person who was to be taken into, and united with the Godhead: if there was any doubt, the Evangelist's application of the latter part of the verse, when the prophecy was accomplished, is sufficient to remove it —"Smite the shepherd, and the sheep shall be scattered."[2] And if the other titles in this prophecy are his, then is this of Ge Ber, or the strong man, also one.

Again, to him only can the famous prophecy in Jeremiah, when rightly translated, in any sense belong; and that also speaks of him under this title—"The Lord hath created a new thing in the earth, a woman shall compass a man"[3]—it ought to be rendered—A woman shall enclose the strong man, or Ge Ber—*i. e.*, shall of herself enclose him, without any human concurrence. Thus a very excellent and learned divine interprets it, adding by way of comment—In this new creation, the "Lord encloseth not Zakor, Ish, or Adam, not *masculus* only, but *Geber, vir fortis*, the valiant or strong man, the grand heroick of the world."[4] And again a little after, where he is shewing the near analogy there is between these words of the prophet, and those spoken by the Angel to the blessed Virgin— "For he shall be great, and shall be called the Son of the Most Highest;"[5] "Is not this," says he, "as

---

[1] עְמִיתִי. [2] Zech. xiii, 7; Matt. xxvi, 31; Mark xiv, 27.
[3] Jer. xxxi, 22. [4] Dr. Jackson, vol. ii, p. 404.
[5] Luke i, 32.

much as *Geber?*"[1]   And in another discourse of his he expressly says of him, that he is "*Geberel, the strength of God.*"[2]

7. Lastly, most of the ancient fathers,[3] and best interpreters,[4] that I have consulted, apply this psalm to him. The learned paraphrast before-mentioned, who collected his paraphrase from Jerom, Augustin, and others, and expounds this psalm for the most part in the manner I do, expressly asserts in his argument to it, that "It treats of the Incarnation of Christ, and the praise of the new law.[5] And Melanchthon the reformer, one of the greatest men of his age, affirms the same more fully—"To what end," says he, "was this preaching ordained? To shew forth Christ, the Son of God. For him is placed a tabernacle in the Church, as for the sun in the heaven: here Christ is manifested, is the fountain of light here, as the sun is the fountain of bodily light."[6]

---

[1] Dr. Jackson, p. 410.   [2] *Ib.* p. 425.
[3] See S. Jerom, Augustin, etc. *Expositionem Patr. Græc. in Psalm.* per Corderium, vol. i, p. 361. Edit. Antverp, 1653.
[4] Jac. Tirinus in his *Comment.* Lugd. 1664, says: "Allegoricè hæc applica Christo incarnato. See also Hammond on this Ps., p. 112.
[5] "Agens de Christi incarnatione, et novæ legis commendatione."—*Synog.*, p. 58.
[6] "Et hæc prædicatio ad quid instituta est? Ad Christum, Filium Dei, monstrandum. Huic ponitur tentorium in ecclesiâ, ut soli in cœlo: hic Christus patefit, hic est fons lucis, ut sol fons est corporalis lucis."—*Argument. Ps. xix*, vol. ii, p. 568. Edit. Wittebergh. 1562.

To which I may add the united sense of many pious and orthodox divines, the compilers of our most excellent liturgy, who undoubtedly would not have appointed it, as they have, for one of the proper psalms upon Christmas day, if they had not thought that, in its full and spiritual sense, it referred to our blessed Lord's incarnation.

To sum up the evidence then by which this interpretation is supported—Christ is the chief or principal subject, the main scope or end of the psalms in general; S. Paul applies the fourth verse of this psalm in a spiritual sense, to the manifestation of him by the preaching of his Apostles; the title of it directs us to apply it to him; the connection of the one part with the other seems to require us to do so; he is eminently styled the sun or light in the prophetical and evangelical writings, and in express terms says so of himself; the characters of the bridegroom and strong man are two of his peculiar titles; and lastly, most of the ancient fathers and best interpreters, that I have consulted, agree with me in the application of it to him. These then are the reasons I promised to lay before you: what regard is to be paid to these arguments, when thrown together and duly considered, I must leave every one to determine for himself; and having thus endeavoured to prove that Christ is the light here spoken of, and that he is represented to us under the image of the material light, I shall now proceed

II. In the second place, to shew the propriety of his being thus represented.

And this, as has been already observed, consists in his doing in the spiritual world what the light does in the natural: we must therefore briefly inquire what the light does there and apply it spiritually as we go along. Light then is appointed to be the author and supporter of animal and vegetable life: this is evident from numberless experiments, from common observation, and from scripture; where we read of "The precious fruits brought forth by the sun, and the precious things put forth by the moon."[1] And is not the operation of the light divine in the moral world equally discernible in its effects? Upon him our spiritual life, our growth in grace, our fruitfulness in good works, our final attainment of perfection wholly depend. Does the natural light in spring-time call forth dead and rotten seeds to the birth, cause naked roots and branches to sprout out afresh, and enliven and renew the face of the earth? So shall it also be in the morning of the resurrection: "For the hour is coming, in the which all that are in the graves shall hear his voice and come forth."[2] Our Lord himself has[3] pointed out this analogy to us, and his Apostle S. Paul circumstantially explained it in the xvth chap. of his 1st epistle to the Corinthians—"But some man will say, How are the dead raised up, and with what bodies do they come? Thou fool, that which thou sowest is not quickened except it die; and that

---

[1] Deut. xxxiii, 14.   [2] John v, 28.   [3] Matth. xii, 25.

which thou sowest, thou sowest not that body which shall be, but bare grain, it may chance, of wheat, or some other grain; but God giveth it a body as it hath pleased him."[1] So will it be with our bodies: they must die before they can be quickened, be sown in corruption ere they can be raised in incorruption, shall be sown bare natural bodies, be raised spiritual ones: and as the material light is the cause of this resurrection in the natural world, so shall the light divine be in the spiritual. There are many other properties and effects, in which the visible sun resembles the Sun of Righteousness: Leigh has reckoned up some of them in a note of his upon a passage in the Revelations, where the woman, *i.e.*, the Church, is represented as clothed with the sun; his words are pretty remarkable—" Cloathed with the sun, that is, Christ," says he; " he resembleth it in its properties and effects. First, properties— 1. In unity, there is but one sun in the world, and but one Sun of Righteousness in the Church. 2. Light. 3. Purity. 4. Power and sufficiency. Secondly, effects—1. Illuminates. 2. Directs. 3. Refresheth; the righteousness of Christ is imputed to the Church."[2] For most of which assertions he cites authorities from scripture.

Such good grounds then had the primitive fathers for using this image so often when they speak of God, as might be shewn by abundance of quota-

---

[1] Matth. xii, 35, etc.   [2] Pag., 595. Edit. Lond. 1650.

tions: of which kind is the following one from S. Greg. Nazianzen—-"What the sun is with regard to sensible things," says he, "that God is with regard to the intellectual; the one enlightens the visible world, the other the invisible."[1] So reasonable was their custom of worshipping eastward: "Because there the light first ariseth out of darkness, and the day of true knowledge arose, like the sun, upon such as lay buried in ignorance;[2] and because God is styled, and is the true light;"[3] as S. Clemens of Alexandria, and S. Athanasius, teach us to answer those who ask the cause of it: and lastly, so just, as well as beautiful, is the epithet Tertullian gives to the rising light, when he calls it " the type or representative of Christ—' orientem Christi figuram.'"[4]

Having thus shewn, that he is in scripture thus

---

[1] Ὁ περ γάρ ἐστι τοῖς αἰσθητοῖς ἥλιος, τοῦτο τοῖς νοητοῖς Θεὸς ὁ μὲν γὲ δὲ τὸν ὁρώμενον φωτίζει κόσμον, ὁ δὲ τὸν ἀόρατον.—*Orat.* Paris. edit. 1609. Vol. i, p. 374.

[2] Ἐπεὶ δὲ γενεθλίου ἡ μέρας εἰκὼν ἡ ἀνατολὴ, κακεῖθεν τὸ φῶς αὔξεται ἐκ σκότοις λάμψαν τὸ πρῶτον. Ἀλλὰ καὶ τοῖς ἐν ἀγνοια καλινδουμένοις ἀνέτειλε γνώσεως ἀληθείας ἡμέρα, κατὰ λόγεν τοῦ ἥλιου—πρὸς τὴν ἑωθινὸν ἀνατολὴν αἱ ἐυχαί.—Paris edit., 1629, p. 724.

[3] Ὅτι οὐκ ὡς ἐν ἀνατολαῖς περιγραφομένου τοῦ Θεοῦ, κατὰ ἀνατολὰς προσκυνοῦμεν, ἀλλ' ἐπειδὴ ὁ Θεὸς φῶς ἀληθινὸν ἔστί τε καὶ ὀνομάζεται—τουτοχάρω πρὸς τὸ κτιστὸν ἀφορῶντες, οὐκ αὐτὸν ἀλλὰ τὸν ποιητὴν αὐτοῦ προσκυνοῦμεν ἐπ' οὗ λαμπροτέρου στοιχεῖον τὰ τῶν πάντυν στοιχείων καὶ τῶν αἰώνων, Θεὸν γεραιρόντες.— S. Athanasius, ita respondendum Gentibus docet.—*Quæst.* ad Antioch. 37a. Paris, 1627.

[4] Advers. Valentin., c. 3.

styled, and that with the greatest propriety, and so removed all reasonable objections to this interpretation of the psalm, I shall now proceed

III. To give a short paraphrase and comment upon it; that the sense in which I understand it, together with the connection and beauty of this divine composition, may be seen at one view.

But here, as I purpose to give the prophetical sense, and it therefore falls not in with my design to mention any other end that might be intended by this description, besides that of leading us to, and explaining spiritual things by natural; it may be proper, before I proceed, just to observe, that I mean not to exclude their opinion of this psalm who consider it as describing the workmanship of the heavens, and thereby displaying the glory of the Maker: I am far from excluding this sense; however, the plan of this discourse will not here permit me to insist upon it, that, I think, the use I make of it greatly heightens and improves it; since our ideas of the infinite wisdom, power, and goodness of God must be considerably enlarged and exalted if we look upon this magnificent theatre, not only as wonderfully framed and fitted to carry on all its various operations for the benefit of man, without the least disorder or confusion; but, besides this, to instruct him also in the highest kind of knowledge, by giving him a sensible representation of what he could not otherwise apprehend. Having premised this, I return to the paraphrase.

"The heavens declare the glory[1] of God, and the firmament" (or expansion)[2] "sheweth his handy work." The heavens point him out to us, who is styled the glory of God; wherever they extend they shew the great work he was to do. "Day unto day[3] uttereth speech, and night unto night sheweth" (or revealeth)[4] "knowledge." They do this continually; day after day, night after night, do they proclaim it: for as their light never ceases its operation, but shineth forth in the night-time in the moon and stars, so even then do they teach this knowledge, and therefore never cease to teach it. "There is neither speech nor language, their voice is not heard."[5] They have no tongues, no articulate sounds,

---

[1] בבוד אל.   [2] וקיע.

[3] יביע. There is a peculiar beauty and exactness in this expression: it signifies to emit, or send out, as a spring does its water, than which there could not be a more proper one used for the issuing forth of light from the sun, the means by which this knowledge is here said to be conveyed. We meet with this allusion frequently in the heathen writers—

"Αὔγλας πολυδερκέα παγὰν."—Dionys. *Hymnogr.*

"Ποταμοὶ δὲ σέθεν πυρὸς ἀμβρότου
Τίκτουσιν ἀπέρα τὸν ἀμέραν."—*Id.*

"Largus item liquidi fons luminis, ætherius sol,
Inrigat assiduè cœlum candore recenti," etc.—Lucret., lib. v, 282.

"Nam licet hinc mundi patefactum totius unum
Largifluum fontem scatere, atque erumpere flumen
Ex omni mundo——".—*Id. ib.*, 592.

[4] יהוה.   [5] See Job xxv, 3.

as men have, to do this, but still they do it, and to persons taught by revelation to apply it, in a most intelligible manner too, a manner well known to the ancient world, by picture or representation. "Their line is gone out through all the earth, and their words[1] to the end of the world." The instruction they disperse abroad is general and unconfined, they teach it to all alike without distinction; resembling herein the blessed Apostles, whose commission was afterwards the same as theirs, to make known to all nations the Sun of Righteousness.

Hitherto the prophet has only told us what is the subject of their instructive lesson: in the next place he shews more particularly the manner in which they convey it. "In them hath he set a tabernacle for the sun." They do it then by the sun that is placed in them, the lively type or image of the Sun of Righteousness, for whom a tabernacle was also prepared, *i.e.*, his human nature, in the which it pleased him to dwell in the fulness of time; whose amazing progress, and mighty effects in his spiritual kingdom, from the beginning to the end of it, the prophet next goes on to describe by images borrowed from his material representative, adding withal such marks of distinction, as sufficiently determine to whom the description properly belongs.

---

[1] מִלֵּיהֶם—the verb מָלַל (whence מִלָּה, words) is used for expressing the meaning by signs. It has this sense, Prov. vi, 13. מוֹלֵל בְּרַגְלָיו, speaking with his foot.

"Which is as a bridegroom coming out of his chamber, and rejoiceth as a strong man to run a race." As the light of the sun goes out in the morning with inconceivable activity, new and youthful itself, and communicating life and gaiety to all things round it, like a bridegroom in the marriage garment from his chamber to his nuptials; so shall the light divine, the promised bridegroom,[1] visit his Church, clad himself, and cloathing her with that robe of righteousness,[2] which is styled in holy scripture the "marriage garment;" and the joy also his presence shall administer shall, like the benefits of it, be universal. And as that is always ready to run its heavenly race, daily issuing forth with renewed vigour, like an invincible champion still fresh to labour; so likewise shall he[3] rejoice to run his glorious race; shall excel in strength, and his works shall be great and marvellous: he shall triumph over the powers of

---

[1] "Teneo meum Christum etiam in nomine sponsi, de quo psalmus—Ipse tanquam sponsus egrediens de thalamo suo, et à summo cœli profectio ejus, et reversio ejus ad summum usque ejus."—Tertull., *Adv. Marcion.*, lib. iv, c. ii.

[2] "I will greatly rejoice in the Lord, my soul shall be joyful in my God, for he hath cloathed me with the garments of salvation, he hath covered me with the robe of righteousness, as a bridegroom decketh himself with ornaments, and as a bride adorneth herself with her jewels."—Isaiah lxi, 10.

[3] Οὐχὶ τλιὺ ἰχυρον ὡς γίγας δραμεῖν αὐτοῦ, περὶ κριστου λελεγμενην γραφὴν ὁμοίως μεμιμῆσθος νοῶ.—Just. Martyr. *Dial.*, p. 287, edit. Lond.

darkness, shed abroad on all sides his bright beams upon his Church, be her deliverer, her protector, and support, able in every respect to accomplish for her the mighty task he has undertaken. All which is already in some degree, but shall hereafter be most gloriously fulfilled in the person and actions of our blessed Lord: "For the kingdom of heaven" (the gospel-state at his coming) "was like unto a certain king which made a marriage for his son"[1]—but the marriage of the Lamb with the Church triumphant is still to come, and his wife is to be glorified—"She shall be arrayed in fine linen, clean and white, for the fine linen is the righteousness of saints."[2] The "strong man armed" has already been overcome and cast out, and therefore it is evident "that a stronger than he is come upon him"[3]—but he shall hereafter be "cast into the lake of fire and brimstone, and shall be tormented day and night, for ever and ever."[4] For our Lord "must reign till he hath put all enemies under his feet."[5] "His going forth is from the end of the heaven, and his circuit unto the ends of it, and there is nothing hid from the heat thereof." His enlivening rays, like those of the sun, shall take their circuit round the earth, go forth out of Judea into all parts of the habitable world, and there is no corner of it so remote as to be without the reach of their healing influence.

---

[1] Matth. xxii, 2. [2] Rev. xix, 7, 8. [3] Luke xi. 21.
[4] Rev. xx, 10. [5] 1 Cor. xv, 25.

Accordingly the event fully verified the prediction: "The Lord gave the word, great was the company of those that published it."[1] The Apostles went out with an unlimited commission to "teach all nations:" and however many then obeyed not the truth, as many now would not if it was preached to them, because many to whom it is preached do not; or may have since, through their own fault, like the descendants of Adam and Noah, deprived themselves and their posterity of the knowledge of it; yet did the Apostles faithfully execute their commission before the destruction of Jerusalem: of which we have infallible proof in the express declaration of their blessed master, who told them, "This gospel of the kingdom shall be preached in all the world,[2] for a witness unto all nations, and then shall the end come."[3] The Prophet therefore having thus foretold the mission of the Apostles, and the success of their ministry, proceeds in the next place to describe their doctrine; so that what follows is a fine encomium upon the gospel, written with all the simplicity peculiar to the sacred language, and in a strain far surpassing the utmost efforts of human eloquence.

"The law of the Lord is perfect, converting the soul." Changing the whole frame and its sinful af-

---

[1] Psalm lxviii, 11.

[2] See Colos. i, 6-23, where S. Paul affirms this prophecy to have been accomplished.

[3] Matth. xxiv, 14.

fections from bad to good, "from dead works to serve the living God."[1] "The testimony of the Lord is sure, making wise the simple." Giving wisdom to babes only, persons of docible childlike dispositions. "The statutes of the Lord are right, rejoicing the heart; the commandment of the Lord is pure, enlightening the eyes." Communicating sight in a spiritual sense, opening the eyes of the understanding,[2] benighted and lost in error and superstition. "The fear of the Lord is clean, enduring for ever; the judgments of the Lord are true and righteous altogether; more to be desired are they than gold, yea than much fine gold." More than all the treasures upon earth. "Sweeter also than honey or the honeycomb." Sweeter to the soul of the pious believer than the sweetest thing we know of is to the taste.[3] All this, indeed, wants little or no explanation, it being almost impossible not to discern the genuine spirit of Christianity in these expressions, the only true religion[4] that ever was in the world since the fall, by the distinguishing characteristic marks here set upon it. The next verse is differently interpreted, and the words "thy servant" thought by some to be applicable to any true believer whatever: but the Prophet rather seems to be here speak-

---

[1] Heb. ix, 14.   [2] See Ephes. i, 18.   [3] See Prov. xxiv, 13, 14.
[4] The patriarchial religion, and that republished afterwards in writing, with some few additions, by Moses, being one and the same, the former part only of the same merciful dispensation.

ing of himself—"Moreover by them is thy servant warned,[1] and in keeping of them there is great reward." The several parts of this perfect law, hereafter to be published to the whole race of mankind, have been all along my great instructors, the only source of all the knowledge to which thy servant has attained; and I am fully assured, that the blessed fruit of them, when they are duly observed, and have their proper effect, is exceeding glorious, even eternal life. Nor will these expressions be thought too strong for the Prophet to use, if we consider, that "The Old Testament is not contrary to the New, for both in the Old and New Testament everlasting life is offered to mankind by Christ," etc., which are the words of our 7th Article; and what our Church has, upon very good grounds, as I could easily shew would the time permit me, farther asserted in her Homilies concerning pious believers both before and under the law—"Although they were not named Christian men, yet was it a Christian faith that they had, for they looked for all the benefits of God the Father through the merits of Jesus Christ, as we now do: this difference is between them and us, they looked when Christ should come, and we be in the time when he is come; therefore saith S. Augustin, the time indeed is altered and changed, but not the faith: for we have

---

[1] Taught, and that in the clearest and most perspicuous manner, as the word נזהר in the orig. implies.—*Illustratur Pagn.*

both one faith in one Christ."[1] The Prophet then puts up a petition for himself, that this divine law he has been describing may always have its perfect work in him; and ends it, and the psalm, with a particular and emphatical address to the person, whom I suppose to have been all along the subject of his praise. "Let the words of my mouth, and the meditation of my heart, be alway acceptable in thy sight, O Lord, my strength and my redeemer."

Thus have I given you my sentiments of this noble composition; which, I hope, now appears to be perfectly regular, and finely conducted, as complete in the design and management of it, as it is in every other respect. And here let me ask, "What are all the celebrated productions of Grecian or Roman wit, when put into the balance with such compositions as these?" The best of those, upon trial, will be found greatly wanting: the disproportion between them, like the distance between their authors, is infinite; and they will always stand distinguished, those by the alloy of human frailty that runs through every part of them, these by their absolute, divine purity: "For the words of the Lord are pure words"—they alone are so—"as silver tried in a furnace of earth, purified seven times"[2]—*i.e.*, to consummate perfection. Indeed to say the sacred writings far surpass human, is saying little of writings dictated by God

---

[1] *Hom. upon Faith*, 2nd pt., p. 23. Oxford edit.
[2] Psalm xi, 6.

himself; nor should I have mentioned it, but for the conclusion I intended to draw from it; which is, that if the superiority is so apparently theirs, so undoubtedly ought to be the preference: this is generally allowed them when we speak of them, but, in fact, I fear, seldom given; most books being read more than the bible, because they are supposed to furnish better entertainment. But surely the exquisite and finished beauty of this simple psalm is more than sufficient to remove so groundless a prejudice: What a pity is it to see creatures designed for immortality, wasting so much of their time, especially the most vigorous and best part of it, in the pursuit of such knowledge as cannot satisfy, which produces only a short-lived, imaginary pleasure, and, by always disappointing our expectation, but increaseth sorrow;[1] while the sacred repositories of all true knowledge,[2] which alone are able to make us wise unto salvation,[3] engage but a small share of their attention; though the subjects they treat of are the most interesting, the sublimest that can be conceived, the instruction they contain full and satisfactory, the composition and style of them masterly beyond all comparison, and the pleasure the reading of them affords rational, pure, and lasting, such as nothing but the joy they are intended to lead us to can excel!

IV. To conclude, the doctrine arising from the

---

[1] Eccles. i, 18. [2] See Coloss. xi, 3. [3] 2 Tim. iii, 15.

whole is, that "Christ is the light of the world;" the necessary consequence of which must be, that all who follow not him walk in darkness: all other schemes of religion are nothing else but so many delusions, thrown out upon every favourable occasion by our spiritual adversary, to deprive us again of a blessed immortality, as he did at first, by turning us aside from the only way by which we can arrive at it. And the policy of the deceiver has been but too successful in every age of the world: for wherever his inventions have prevailed, or do now prevail, there always in proportion have abounded, and still abound, ignorance, "confusion, and every evil work."[1] Let a serious reflection then upon the misery of those from whom the light of the gospel is hid, make us truly sensible of our happy condition; let us, with hearts full of gratitude, be ever ready to acknowledge the great mercy that has been vouchsafed us; and continually "give thanks unto the Father, which has made us meet to be partakers of the inheritance of the saints in light: who hath delivered us from the power of darkness, and hath translated us into the kingdom of his dear Son, in whom we have redemption through his blood, even the forgiveness of sins."[2] But let us not stop here; let us, who believe this great and comfortable truth, do all that we are able for the preservation and support of it. Let those, therefore, who are entrusted with the

---

[1] Jam. iii, 16. [2] Coloss. i, 12, etc.

education of youth, take care before all things to lay open to them the inexhaustible treasures of heavenly wisdom, to read over with them and expound the sacred oracles; that by these means the faith, sown early in their hearts, may increase with their years, and by the time they are called out into the world, be able to stand firm against every blast of opposition. And let all who are sent to these learned societies for instruction, those especially who enjoy the liberality of their founders and benefactors, use them to that pious end for which they were instituted and endowed; always remembering, that it has ever been the distinguished honour of this place, to have "contended earnestly for the faith, which was once delivered to the saints."[1] They have now a happy opportunity, in this their retirement and freedom from worldly cares and business, to lay in such a store of divine knowledge, as will be a never failing source of joy and consolation, a sure guide and security to them through the whole course of their lives, and of infinite benefit to themselves and others. Let them study then to make daily improvements in this blessed knowledge, which they will carry with them beyond the grave, and whatever situation they shall hereafter be placed in, do their utmost to communicate and to promote it. But let those who are to be set apart for this labour of love, whose proper and more immediate office it will be to for-

---

[1] Jude 3.

ward the salvation of men, be particularly careful to employ this season to the best advantage. The present time, days "of rebuke and blasphemy!"[1] call for the utmost industry and application in the Christian ministry: let them now therefore make a wise and early provision for the warfare in which they are to engage; attentively read, and frequently meditate upon the sacred pages they are to explain; let those who have abilities apply themselves to the languages in which they are written, consider the relation of each part to the whole, the spiritual intention, as well as literal sense of every passage, the full force and weight of every expression; constantly imploring the direction of the Holy Spirit who dictated them, without whose assistance they can never be thoroughly understood. And when they are commissioned to preach the word, let them do it with sincerity, with becoming resolution, and unwearied diligence; "Be instant in season, and out of season,"[2] as ready to guide the ignorant and unstable, as the enemies of the cross are to mislead them, as industrious to save men's souls, as they are to destroy them: this is a most charitable and glorious work; it is to enlarge our blessed master's kingdom, to be "labourers together with God."[3] And the reward is as glorious as the work itself; for "they that be wise" (or "teachers," as it is in the marginal reading) "shall shine forth as the brightness of the firmament,

---

[1] 2 Kings xix, 3. [2] 2 Tim. iv, 2. [3] 1 Cor. iii, 9.

and they that turn many to righteousness, as the stars for ever and ever."[1] Finally, my brethren, let us all, whatever our station or profession may be, be careful to "add to" our "faith virtue,"[2] to shew forth the excellency of our religion by the holiness of our lives: this will be the best recommendation of it to others, and without this it will not profit ourselves—Our "God is light, and in him is no darkness at all; if we say that we have fellowship with him, and walk in darkness, we lie, and do not the truth: but if we walk in the light, as he is in the light, we have fellowship one with another, and the blood of Jesus Christ his Son cleanseth us from all sin."[3] In a word then, let us "walk as children of light,"[4] making daily preparation, by acquiring still more refined and heavenly dispositions, for that perfect state of bliss which is to be our portion hereafter; for to those who so walk in the Jerusalem that is below, shall it be given to walk for ever in the "light" of the "Lord God,"[5] and of the "Lamb,"[5] in the light of Jerusalem that is above.

To which blessed place God, of his infinite mercy, bring us all, through the merits and intercession of Jesus Christ; to whom, with the Father, and the Holy Spirit, the adorable and eternal Trinity, be glory in the Church throughout all ages, world without end. Amen.

---

[1] Dan. xii, 3.   [2] 2 Pet. i, 5.   [3] 1 Ep. John i, 5.
[4] Ephes v, 8.   [5] Rev. xxi, 23; xxii, 5.

A SEASONABLE ADMONITION

TO THE CHURCH OF ENGLAND.

A SERMON

PREACHED BEFORE THE UNIVERSITY OF OXFORD,

AT

ST. MARY'S,

ON THE TWENTY-NINTH OF MAY, 1751.

"And what I say unto you, I say unto all, Watch."—MARK xiii, 37.
"Watch ye, stand fast in the faith."—1 COR. xvi, 13.
"Behold, I come quickly: hold that fast, which thou hast, that no man take thy crown."
Our Lord to the Church in Philadelphia.—REV. iii, 11.

OXFORD:

PRINTED AT THE THEATRE FOR SACKVILLE PARKER, AND
E. WITHERS, AT THE SEVEN STARS, NEAR TEMPLE BAR.
MDCCLV.

Imprimatur,

GEO. HUDDESFORD,

Vice-Can. Oxon.

Mar. 12, 1755.

PREFACE

TO THE

CHURCH OF ENGLAND.

My beloved brethren,—The following discourse, not having been published at the time it was preached, was not afterwards intended for the press; but the reasons, which then induced me to choose the subject, here considered, for the day's meditation, and to consider it in the manner I have done, are now become much stronger motives to the publication of my sentiments; inattention and indifference to the things of God increasing more and more throughout the land, and infidelity thence taking occasion daily to insinuate its mortal venom into the very vitals of Christianity! And shall the love of Christ, in the hearts of his ministers, be less active to save his people, than the malice of Satan in the hearts of his enemies, so evidently is to destroy them? God forbid! No—it is our duty to speak, even though we are not heard; to proclaim the glad tidings of peace, though men will remain at enmity with God; to call off their grovelling attention from earthly to spiritual pursuits, though they should still prefer earth to heaven, transitory vanities to eternal glory; to shew them the way, and the truth, and the life, even the Lord Jesus Christ, who, and who only, is all these,[1] though they should perversely wander on still in the wilderness of their own way, through all the mazes of error, into an endless death. And in a time of spiritual famine and distress, we should do this with the more assiduity ; it is a constant labor of love, but eminently so at such a season ; he that sees another's danger, and warns him not of it, cannot possibly love him. Now all, that is here proposed to you, my brethren, flows from this principle entirely, from the love of Christ, and the love of you, for his sake. If I loved not him, I should not be zealous for his glory—I should hold my peace ; if I loved not you, I should not be zealous for your salvation—I could then see you perish with indifference. Wherefore, I beseech you, bear with me who love you, and suffer while it is to day, the word of exhortation. You cannot but be sensible surely, upon reflection, that the generality of you are very far from God ; chiefly, if not wholly, intent upon the pleasures and interests of this world ; regardless of the things beyond it, which are only seen with the eye of faith ; almost entirely unacquainted with the evidence of God's word ; and having little or no experience of the effects of his religion. Hence it is, that the things designed for

---

[1] John xiv, 6.

your knowledge, are so dark and difficult to be understood; you want that spiritual discernment, without which, the Apostle tells you, you cannot see them.[1] Hence the great truths of our most holy faith :—1. The personality in the godhead. 2. The grace superadded to the blessed sacraments. 3. The spiritual sense of the bible. 4. Justification in Christ alone, by faith only, without any works that we can do towards it, &c. Hence likewise all the divine institutions thereof : Those, 1. Of holy matrimony. 2. Of episcopacy. 3. Of an order of persons separated to officiate, under their authority, in holy things. 4. Of Ecclesiastical censures and wholesome discipline, to restrain destructive heresies, carnal schisms, and ungodliness, (for take away the government and discipline of a church, and her doctrines and devotion will soon follow after)—these, I say, and in a word, all divine things whatever, are generally esteemed subjects of doubtful disputation, if not totally disbelieved : though in the instances above mentioned, it is demonstrable from holy scripture (the only guide in spiritual matters, which are not objects of sense), that, 1. There are three, that bear record in heaven, the Father, the Word, and the Holy Ghost, and these three are one;[2] that, thus saith the Lord, "cursed (is) the man, that trust-teth in man";[3] (but we trust in Christ),[4] and that

---

[1] 1 Cor. ii, 14. [2] 1 John v. 7. [3] Jer. xvii, 5.
[4] Matth. xii, 21 ; Ephes. i, 12, 13.

none (no man) can by any means redeem (his) brother, or give to God a ransom for him;[1] (but we are redeemed by Christ,[2] and he is our ransom).[3] Wherefore our Lord Christ must be very God, as well as very man, else were our religion a self contradiction, and our worship idolatry; that a spiritual creation is as much a work of Almighty power, as a natural one, and the Holy Spirit, in the work of our sanctification, creates a clean heart, and renews a right spirit within us.[4] That, 2. "Except a man be born of water and the Spirit, he cannot enter into the kingdom of God;"[5] and, "Except ye eat the flesh of the Son of Man, and drink his blood, ye have no life in you"—"Whoso eateth my flesh and drinketh my blood, hath eternal life"—"He that eateth of this bread shall live for ever."[6] The external cleansing of the laver cannot wash away sin; nor the perishable substance of the bread and wine keep the body from decay, much less preserve that and the soul unto everlasting life: only the eternal spirit, accompanying the outward rite with almighty power, can, by moving upon the face of the waters, in this new or spiritual creation, and applying the body and blood of Christ to the souls of believers, "Purge the conscience from dead works to serve the

---

[1] Ps. xlix, 7. [2] Coloss. i, 14; Heb. ix, 12; Rev. v, 9. [3] Job xxxiii, 24; Hosea xiii, 14; Matthew xx, 28; 1 Tim. ii, 6. [4] Ps. li, 10, 11; civ, 30; Tit. iii, 5. [5] John. iii, 5. [6] John vi, 53, 54, 58.

living God,"[1] or support that life in man which is not sustained by bread.[2] Nay, that what we call sacraments must be visible signs of invisible things, or they must cease to be sacraments, for "a sacrament is an outward or visible sign of an inward and spiritual grace"—yea, and "'a means' too whereby we receive the same". That, 3. The holy scriptures, unless spiritually interpreted, are like the mere elements in the sacraments, a dead and killing letter,[3] as unable to give life to the devout reader, as those elements are to do the same to the faithful receiver. And that, 4. The Apostle saith—"Knowing that a man is not justified by the works of the law, but by the faith of Jesus Christ, even we have believed in Jesus Christ, that we might be justified by the faith of Christ, and not by the works of the law—for by the works of the law shall no flesh be justified".[4] For that would make us, in part, our own Saviours and justifiers, whereas Christ hath suffered in our stead, and done and merited for us sinners, what we could not do or merit for ourselves; wherefore high reason is there, that it should be, as the divine scriptures affirm, "Not of him that willeth, nor of him that runneth, but of God that showeth mercy".[5] After we are justified, we may, and ought to work indeed under sanctifying grace; but yet, no work that proceedeth of grace lays claim to any merit

---

[1] Heb. ix, 14. [2] Deut. viii, 3; Matth. iv, 4. [3] 2 Cor. iii, 6.
[4] Gal. ii, 16. [5] Rom. ix, 16.

of its own, any reward as of debt, but humbly seeks acceptance through his merits, by whose divine power it was wrought.

That with regard to the other point, the divine institutions above spoken of,—1. The Lord God brought the first woman in Paradise, unto the man in person,[1] and still joins man and wife by divinely-delegated power, which is therefore as much his act and deed, as if he did it in person.[2] That, 2. The divinely-inspired Apostles, who were themselves appointed by Christ, appointed bishops for their successors; and that no man taketh the honour of this office, either of the high priesthood, or episcopacy (which is the same)—no not the Man Christ himself, without being "called of God,"[3] *i.e.*, appointed by the power, and in the method of his divine institution, who accordingly called (or so appointed) the first-born under the patriarchal state, the family of Aaron under the law, and the Apostles, and their duly consecrated successors under the gospel: Korah, Dathan, and Abiram, for taking it to themselves, went down alive into the pit.[4] That, 3. With regard to the priesthood, Moses, having frequently recorded God's appointment of the first-born, to officiate in the then-united character of the high priesthood, and the priesthood, relates the re-institution of these holy offices, when separated, in the most circumstantial manner possible—that

---

[1] Gen. ii, 22.   [2] Matth. xix, 6.   [3] Hebr. v, 4, 5.
[4] Numb. xvi, 3, 5, 32, 33, 40.

having first, by divine direction, consecrated Aaron himself, he then immediately, by the same divine commission, consecrated the sons of Aaron, the priests, *i.e.*, as the original words for consecrated signify, he perfected or fully-impowered them (therefore they had no power of themselves) to minister in holy things, in the sight, *i.e.*, under the episcopacy, inspection, or authority of Aaron their father."[1] And that St. Paul expressly declares, for our purpose, that he left one of the bishops, he had appointed, in Crete, to ordain elders or presbyters (*i.e.* priests) in every city, "Even," says the Apostle, "as I had appointed thee."[2] Heaping up to themselves teachers, is a mark set by the same Apostle upon such as "will not endure sound doctrine," but follow "after their own lusts—having itching ears;"[3] and is one of the highest crimes a man can be guilty of against the spirit of unity. And 4. Lastly, with regard to discipline, that our Lord saith—"Whoever shall neglect to hear the Church, let him be unto thee as an heathen man and a publican" (*i.e.*, cut off by excommunication from all the privileges of the gospel) adding very remarkably, in the words immediately following, his own divine ratification of all duly-inflicted acts of discipline—"Verily I say unto you, whatsoever ye shall bind on earth, shall be bound in heaven, and whatsoever ye shall loose on earth, shall be loosed in heaven."[4] To which

---

[1] Exod. xxix; Levit. viii; Numb. iii, 3, 4.   [2] 2 Tit. i, 5.
[3] 2 Tim. iv, 3.   [4] Matth. xviii, 17, 18.

divinely-instituted authority the Apostle doubtless refers in his direction both to Timothy and Titus: "Them that sin, rebuke before all, that others also may fear;"[1] "these things speak, and exhort, and rebuke with all authority—let no man despise thee."[2] Though all these, and others that might be mentioned (as might be more fully shewn) are, I say, so clear beyond all contradiction—yet, how few, called Christians, are at all acquainted with them; how many (I trust, in ignorance) dispute, or perhaps entirely disbelieve them? And how openly are they, with the pen and tongue, yea, and with what impunity, blasphemed? And yet, they are fundamental articles of the Christian religion. Though we hear so little of them, wherever we go, and with whomsoever we converse, they are the things we were born to know; they are the only things, the knowledge of which will profit us; the only knowledge that we shall carry beyond the grave; the only wisdom that leads to heaven. Thus far gone out of the way, and dead to the spiritual things of the city that is above, you rest satisfied with earthly things, and mere external observances; as if faith which worketh by love,[3] and hope, the anchor of the soul,[4] as if spiritual persons, things, and operations were mere matters of opinion, no way essential to salvation; as if to follow Israel in her unbelief, was the path to that rest, which

---

[1] 1 Tim. v, 20. [2] Tit. ii, 15. [3] Gal. v, 6. [4] Heb. vi, 19.

she fell short of because of unbelief,[1] or taking hold of the law (which you cannot perform) without the end thereof (which is and ever was Christ),[2] was the way now to the privileges of the gospel. And yet, we profess, as all true Christians must profess, yea, and what is more, must experience, that we are risen with Christ,[3] (risen from the death of sin to the new life of righteousness in him,)[4] and that, in consequence of this our spiritual resurrection (the pledge or earnest of our bodily resurrection), we set our affections on things above, and not (as we used to do) on things on the earth.[5] And he that does so is indeed a Christian. But are the generality of you in this state? Ask your own hearts the question, and let me intreat you to improve the testimony they shall give you to your soul's health. Beloved, if our heart (tried by God's word) condemn us not, then have we confidence towards God.[6] Otherwise, make haste to escape; you know not the extreme danger of an hour's delay; "For in such an hour as you think not, the Son of Man cometh":[7] not only to judge the world, but to execute vengeance, in the mean season, upon all apostate churches, as he said —"I will come unto thee quickly, and will remove thy candlestick out of his place, except thou repent."[8] How much longer space his divine forbearance will allow us for repentance—or how soon we, whom he

---

[1] Heb. iii, 19.   [2] Rom. x, 4; Heb. xiii, 8.   [3] Coloss. iii, 1.
[4] Rom. vi, the whole chapter.   [5] Coloss. iii, 2.
[6] 1 John iii, 21.   [7] Matth. xxiv, 44.   [8] Rev. ii, 5.

yet graciously refers to the churches he has already destroyed for an example, may, by his just judgement, become ourselves a sad example to others—I dare not to take upon me to conjecture; but sure I am, the signs of the times, compared with the histories of those that are past, afford abundant matter for the most melancholy reflection. The following sheets, I may hope, if read with attention and without prejudice, will, by the blessing of God, awaken some out of the dangerous slumber that is fallen upon them, which so shuts up their inward senses against all spiritual discernment, and habitually deadens their affections to the things of God. As the arguments, here offered, were of use to myself, I may reasonably hope they will be of some benefit to others; and therefore no imperfection of mine, in the execution of my design, could prevail with me to withhold it any longer from them. What is wanting in the writer, will be fully made up by accompanying grace to him that reads it with sincerity. And I most earnestly beseech our Lord Jesus Christ, who is the power of God, and the wisdom of God,[1] to make this humble attempt of one of the meanest of his servants, as well as its author, what, without his divine blessing upon them, neither can be of themselves—effectual instruments in his hand for the enlargement of his kingdom, *i.e.*, for the further display of his glory, and the salvation of his people.

GEORGE WATSON.

---

[1] 1 Cor. i, 24.

A SEASONABLE ADMONITION

TO THE

CHURCH OF ENGLAND.

A SERMON.

St. Jude 5.

I will therefore put you in remembrance, though ye once knew this, how that the Lord, having saved the people out of the land of Egypt, afterward destroyed them that believed not.

The design of this awakening admonition, as indeed of the whole epistle where it occurs, was to put the Christian Churches upon their guard in a time of manifest danger, and thereby prevent the ruinous consequences of a general apostasy. The days, foretold by our Lord and his apostles, were now accomplished; the mystery of iniquity, they spake of, had begun to take effect; there were certain men crept in unawares (the Greek word is παρεισεδυσαν, had entered in a by-way, made themselves teachers, without a regular divinely-instituted appointment), whose tenets were directly opposite to the saving doctrines they had received; and therefore, whatever they might pretend, calculated only to introduce anarchy and confusion, to rob the Church of its peace both here and hereafter. A case of so desperate a nature required a timely interposition, and a more powerful one there could not have been than this of our Apostle. What he hath written upon this occasion is full of divine energy; the sentiments have in them all the depth and majesty that is peculiar to the divine writings; and the expressions, with which they are clothed, are the inimitable language of the Spirit of God. The argument, he here uses for the establishment of the faithful, is of all others the most awful and affecting; it involves in it the whole stupendous scheme of God's immutable councils, with respect to all whom he created to be partakers of his glory; of mercy to all, who would, upon trial, accept of it, and of judgement, without mercy, to all who, in their state of probation, would finally reject it; in a word, the vast and comprehensive plan, which God saw to be good, and therefore decreed before all time, and the invariable method of his administration in time, to execute and accomplish it. The part of it we are now to consider, is that which relates to his Church, here exemplified in the miraculous deliverance of his people out of Egypt, and the judgements that afterwards befell them for their incorrigible impenitence. This argument is much insisted upon by the Apostles; they frequently repeat it, they recommend it with earnestness; believers, even in those earlier and better times, not being so attentive to the works of God in his dealings with Israel, as was necessary for their own welfare and security. This is implied by our Apostle in the former member of the text—"I will therefore" (says he) " put you in remembrance, though ye once knew this." The fact itself they cannot well be supposed to have forgotten ; the bible was the chief and almost only study of Christians in those days ; they were sensible of its incomparable excellence, and most thankfully and devoutly gave the preference where it is due. The Apostle's meaning therefore must be, that they had (undesignedly, I question not) neglected to make the proper use of the above-mentioned history; considered it indeed as an infallible relation of great and glorious transactions, wherein the almighty power and loving kindness of Jehovah were most marvellously displayed, and for which his name was to be praised throughout all succeeding generations; but they did not reflect, how nearly they were concerned in it; they applied it not to themselves; and therefore wanted, in the circumstances they then were, the most effectual restraint that could be laid upon them, the best means to prevent their falling after the same example of unbelief. Of this application then the Apostle reminds them, and his words are of the same import with those of St. Paul to the Corinthians—" Now all these things happened unto them for ensamples" (Gr. τυποι, types), " and they are written for our admonition, upon whom the ends of the world are come." And then follows the application to that Church, in as express terms as possible—" Wherefore, let him, that thinketh he standeth, take heed, lest he fall."[1]

The Apostle's words then, compared with those of St. Paul, contain this great and important truth, to which it is the duty of all, for whose instruction it was written, to give a serious and frequent attention; namely, that God's proceedings with the Israelites, with regard to national visitations, are a type or figure of his proceedings with his Church in all ages, to the end of the world.—For the full and clear illustration of which point, I shall in the following discourse,

I. Enquire into the grounds and reasons of the truth here asserted.

II. Prove the general assertion by an induction of particulars; in which an opportunity will be given me of insisting more especially upon God's mercies to this Church and nation, as vouchsafed upon this day.

III. Offer some short reflections upon the whole to your consideration; wherein it will appear, what qualifications are requisite on our part for the religious celebration of this day's solemnity. I am

I. To enquire into the grounds or reasons of the truth here asserted. And those undoubtedly are, 1. That the scheme of God's government (as has been observed) is an universal, not partial one; and 2. The deliverance, here referred to, the greatest

---

[1] 1 Cor. x, 11, 12.

temporal deliverance that ever was wrought for the Church. With regard to the first, the scheme of the divine administration, it must be universal, because it is founded and proceeds upon the plan of redemption, concerning which the prophet declares, that "The Lord (is) good to all, and his tender mercies (are) over all his works";[1] and the Apostles, that "Jesus Christ is the propitiation for our sins, and not for ours only, but also (for the sins) of the whole world";[2] "That God is no respecter of persons, but in every nation, he that feareth him, and worketh righteousness, is accepted with him."[3] The terms of acceptance then are open to all, and if all are not partakers of the inestimable benefit that was intended for all, it is not to be imputed to any defect in the means of salvation, any partiality in God, but to an obstinate and final resistance of every overture of grace, or an apostacy from the faith, after we have been enlightened. The terms of acceptance you have just now heard—"He that feareth God and worketh righteousness, is accepted." From which words I hope to convince you, that the divine author of our salvation, the inexhaustible fountain of all mercy and love, has never yet finally deserted, and never will desert any individual man, or society of men, that have not first deserted him finally and impenitently. Now, by the "fear of God" (when all the passages where the word occurs are

---

[1] Ps. cxlv, 9.   [2] 1 John ii, 2.   [3] Acts x, 34, 35.

compared together) is plainly signified—an awful sense of his immutable justice, as the sure avenger of unexpiated sin: it has evidently this signification in those words of our Saviour, "But I will forewarn you whom you shall fear: fear him, which, after he hath killed, hath power to cast into hell, yea, I say unto you, fear him."[1] Whoever has this fear in himself will, with joy and thankfulness of heart, "lay hold of the hope that is set before him;" and the same principle will preserve him, that retains it, stedfast in this hope, till the love of God be made perfect in him, and "perfect love casteth out fear." Thus is the well-grounded fear of God essentially connected with an humble desire of his mercy, and therefore "His mercy is on them that fear him from generation to generation."[2] We are next to consider, what it is to work righteousness. And here it must be remembered, that the sacred scriptures positively declare that no son of fallen Adam hath any righteousness of his own, and what righteousness then can he work of himself? "All our righteousnesses are as filthy rags;"[3] and it is written, "There is none righteous, no not one."[4] The righteousness therefore here spoken of must be the Redeemer's righteousness, who is the end of the law for righteousness to every one that believeth; *i.e.*, who has fulfilled the all-perfect law of God for us, as well as paid the satisfaction for our transgression of it; neither of

---

[1] Luke xii, 5.
[2] Luke i, 50.
[3] Isaiah lxiv, 6.
[4] Rom. iii, 10.

which we sinners could do for ourselves; and now by his Holy Spirit enables our faith in him to put forth those acceptable fruits of righteousness in grace, which, by reason of sin, we never more could have produced by nature. But from his divine inexhaustible store all man's righteousness is derived; and it is called "our righteousness" in holy scripture, because it is first imputed and then given to us, not because it is our own, as of ourselves, for it is the gift of God in Christ: only we are free, whether we will accept of it, or trust to our own,—and upon our choice our salvation depends.

By faith then it is, and by faith only, that man can work righteousness as it is witnessed of the saints of old—by faith they wrought righteousness[1]—Whosoever will accept of righteousness upon these terms, may work righteousness again, and every son of Adam, that does so accept of it, is accepted with God—No soul, that ever applied through Christ for it, was ever rejected. From the terms of our acceptance then, thus explained by the obvious sense of the words in holy writ, there necessarily arises the following inference, namely, that God, having determined to save fallen man by Jesus Christ, considers the whole race of Adam in this relation. Jehovah (says Isaiah) is well pleased for his righteousness sake;[2] *i.e.*, his wrath is appeased, and therefore by his good-will restored to mankind for the sake of

---

[1] Heb. xi, 33.   [2] Isaiah xlii, 21.

Christ's righteousness. As many therefore, as seek by faith for justification in Christ, come under the terms and receive the benefit. If the whole race of Adam would have done so, as he did, the whole race would have been accepted; a man cannot exclude himself, but by voluntarily disqualifying himself; and according to their own future choice fore-known of God, before the foundation of the world,[1] God hath regulated his proceedings with men from the beginning, and will do so to the end. To shew this in the manner it ought to be done, it would be necessary to transcribe a complete history of the true religion, and the false, in all its branches, from the fall to these our days; but I am obliged to confine myself to a few instances, which will, I hope, be sufficient. Abel, then, we read, was accepted, and Cain rejected. But St. Paul informs us that Abel was a believer;[2] he offered by faith. And St. Jude, that Cain was an apostate; for speaking of the apostate hereticks of his time, whom he styles, twice dead, *i.e.*, not only born, as all originally are, in a state of everlasting death, but now likewise cut off by their apostacy from the life which is in Christ, he says, "they have gone in the way of Cain."[3] Again; God hated Esau, and loved Jacob. But Esau, St. Paul declares, was an infidel and profane person, who

---

[1] "For whom he did foreknow, he also did predestinate"—to what? It follows—"to be conformed to the image of his Son," etc.—Rom. viii, 29.

[2] Heb. xi, 4.   [3] Jude — 11.

for one morsel of meat (to satisfy a little temporal want) sold his birthright;[1] and therewith not only the kingdom and the priesthood, which were annexed to it, but all his hopes, and for all he knew to the contrary, those of mankind too, in the Messiah: he afterwards married into an heathen family.[2] But Jacob is enrolled amongst the illustrious worthies, who obtained a good report through faith;[3] and being heir of the faith of Abraham, he became also heir of the promise. Again; to Pharaoh the scripture saith, "even for this same purpose I have raised thee up" (*i.e.*, to the throne, not to life) " that I might shew my power in thee," etc., and the same scripture saith, that "his heart was hardened."[4] But the same scripture saith, likewise, he hardened his own heart;[5] in further evidence of which, let us hear him speak of himself—"Who is Jehovah," says he, "that I should obey his voice?" His insolence was incorrigible, his pride above all conviction. A long series of most astonishing and acknowledged miracles could not humble him; he pressed on to destruction, with one of the greatest before his eyes; a fitter example of divine justice cannot well, I think, be conceived!

Thus it is with individuals then, but it may be asked, is it so also with societies? as if societies did not consist of individuals, and the whole could be deprived of God's favour, while the part enjoy it, or

---

[1] Heb. xii, 16.   [2] Gen. xxvi, 34.   [3] Heb. xi, 21.
[4] Exod. ix, 16-35. Compare with Romans ix, 17, 18.
[5] Exod. ix, 34.

the whole enjoy it, when the parts have forfeited it! Here let me repeat, that all God's mercies to individuals, since the fall, have been bestowed through the alone merits and intercession of Christ: at whatever time they are finally withdrawn, whether from individuals or communities, which they never are till there is no room for amendment, then, and not till then, individuals are appointed to everlasting destruction, and communities to temporal; exclusion from the presence of God becomes necessary in the one case, and excision in the other. To confirm this likewise briefly by an example. That the Lord loved Israel and hated Canaan, will readily be allowed. Now if it shall appear, that his dealings with them were as impartial, as with the above-mentioned individuals, the conclusion will be the same here as there. The Israelites were the descendants of the father of the faithful, they professed the true religion in an idolatrous world, and retained it, as a nation, when the Canaanites had rejected it. God, foreseeing this, promised Abram to put his seed in possession of the land of Canaan, and fulfilled his promise at the time appointed. But here, behold the long-suffering of God in the wide interval between the promise and its completion, with the merciful reason he himself has assigned for it! "But in the fourth generation" (not before) "they shall come hither again, for the iniquity of the Amorites is not yet full".[1]

---

[1] Gen. xv, 16.

What tender love is here shewn to a sinful people! What more could have been done for Israel! When their day of vengeance approached, he delivered Israel out of Egypt; but he suffered Israel to abuse his mercy, no more than the Amorites. As the apostacy of the former was not yet general, so neither was their destruction; but by various visitations he cut them off which believed not; the generation that saw his miracles in Egypt fell in their passage through the wilderness, all but Joshua and Caleb, who were eminent for their faith; and how he dealt with their posterity, after their settlement, we shall soon have occasion to mention. I will only add here the declarations of Moses, very apposite to the present purpose, and which the event proved to be prophetical—"And it shall be, if thou do at all forget the Lord thy God, and walk after other gods, and serve them and worship them; I testify against you this day, that ye shall surely perish; as the nations, which the Lord destroyeth before your face, so shall ye perish."[1] And in another place he says, that "if they would not observe to do all the words of the law, God would bring upon them all the diseases of Egypt."[2]

The impartiality of God's dealings with mankind being thus established, Israel will appear to be the fittest pattern that could be given to succeeding generations, because 2dly, their deliverance was

---

[1] Deut. viii, 19. [2] Deut. xxviii, 58.

the greatest temporal deliverance that ever was wrought for the Church. The circumstances of time and place, as well as the typical respect this great event was to have to man's spiritual deliverance, required an extraordinary exertion of divine power—"Marvellous things therefore God did for them in the land of Egypt, in the field of Zoan."[1]—"He brought them forth out of Egypt, with a mighty hand, and with an out-stretched arm, and with great terribleness, and with signs, and with wonders."[2] Now the meritorious cause of his mercies being the same to all, if, notwithstanding such a salvation, so mightily conducted, so gloriously accomplished, he afterward destroyed them that believed not, the Church, in all future ages, would herein best discern the immutability of his proceedings. That they have been invariably the same with the Church in future ages, is the general assertion I am to prove.

II. By an induction of particulars; in which an opportunity will be given me of insisting more especially upon God's mercies to this Church and nation, vouchsafed as upon this day. And I. God did unto the Israelites, after their settlement in Canaan, as he had done unto their forefathers. To pass over here their divers visitations, which were sent in mercy to them, as to other nations, to call them to repentance, their many less remarkable captivities under the Judges, and the greater ones

---

[1] Ps. lxxviii, 12.   [2] Deut. xxvi, 8.

of the Ten Tribes, after their revolt from the house of David, let us consider only the famous captivity of Judah and their final dispersion. The former of these, together with the cause of it, you have recorded by the inspired historian, at the conclusion of the Books of Chronicles—"Moreover," says he, "all the chief of the priests, and the people, transgressed very much, after all the abominations of the heathen, and polluted the House of the Lord, which he had hallowed in Jerusalem. And the Lord God of their fathers sent to them by his messengers, rising betimes and sending, because he had compassion on his people and on his dwelling-place: but they mocked the messengers of God, and despised his words, and misused his Prophets, until the wrath of the Lord arose against his people, till there was no remedy. Therefore he brought upon them the king of the Chaldees."[1] This is too plain to need any comment. But the promises of God, not yet fulfilled, required Judah's restoration; and their affliction had so humbled them, as to make them again proper objects of his mercy—"By the rivers of Babylon there they sat down, yea, they wept when they remembered Zion."[2] Thus they came once more under the terms of acceptance. Moses had expressly said, that if they would return at any time unto the Lord their God, he would return, and gather them from all the nations whither he had

---

[1] 2 Chron. xxxvi, 14.   [2] Ps. cxxxvii, 1.

scattered them—"The Lord therefore was favourable to his land, and brought back the captivity of Jacob."[1] But they again rebelled against the Lord their God, again resisted the Holy Ghost, as their fathers had done, who "killed the prophets, and stoned them that were sent unto them."[2] So they were again given up to a judicial blindness, which led them at length to fill up the measure of their fathers by crucifying the prince of life, and persecuting Christianity.[3] Since which his imprecated blood has laid heavy upon them; he brought the Roman abomination of desolation into his holy place, and, by a most unparalleled destruction, overthrew their city and temple, dispersing the remnant to the four winds of heaven. In this deplorable state have they now continued near 1700 years, and shall continue so, till they acknowledge him whom they crucified— They shall see him no more till they shall say, "Blessed (is) he that cometh in the name of the Lord;"[4] *i.e.*, till they shall acknowledge him for their Messiah; those who did believe in him at his coming having acknowledged him by this title.[5] "Jerusalem shall be trodden down of the Gentiles, until the times of the Gentiles be fulfilled;"[6] *i.e.*, according to St. Paul's interpretation, "until the fulness of the Gentiles be come in."[7] Observe here, the Jews were rejected, because they rejected the

---

[1] Ps. lxxxv, 1.   [2] Matth. xxiii, 37.   [3] 1 Thess. ii, 15, 16.
[4] Matth. xxiii, 39.   [5] Matth. xxi, 9.
[6] Luke xxi, 24.   [7] Rom. xi, 25.

Messiah; he was preached to the Gentiles, because the Gentiles were ready to receive him:—but when the Gentiles shall likewise reject him, and his people be willing to receive him, the Gentiles shall be rejected, and he shall return to his people. Well might he expostulate with them by the mouth of his holy prophet, "O house of Israel, are not my ways equal, are not your ways unequal?"[1]

2ndly. God has done unto the Christian Churches as he did unto the Jewish. This is too copious a subject to have a particular consideration now; but a general account of the Eastern Churches, the seven especially named in the Revelations, with the total subversion of the empire itself, will, 'tis presumed, be as full an evidence as will here be expected. And the more so, as the things, recorded of those seven Churches, comprehend in them every possible state, in which any Church can be; and were therefore recorded, that they might be a standing lesson to all Churches, in the ages to come, an invariable standard of our Lord's dealings with all, even to the end of the world. Now the fate of all these has long been determined; the predictions of our Lord concerning them have had an end; and that decisive one sent to the Church in Ephesus been fulfilled in all—"Remember, therefore," said he to her, "from whence thou art fallen, and repent, and do the first works, or else I will come unto thee quickly, and

---

[1] Ezek. xviii, 29.

will remove thy candlestick out of his place, except thou repent."[1] The time of their visitation then being past and allowed, we have only to inquire into the occasion of it, whether they likewise despised the long-suffering of God, and perished because of unbelief. It is plain from the Epistles, written by our Lord's direction, to the angels or bishops of these Churches, and therein to the Churches themselves, that most of them were even then declining towards apostasy. "He that hath an ear, let him hear what the spirit there saith to the Churches." The Church in Ephesus, he saith, "had left her first love;"[2] the Church in Pergamus had them that "held the doctrine of Balaam, who taught Balac to cast a stumbling-block before the children of Israel, to eat things sacrificed unto idols, and to commit fornication;" and of the Nicholaitans, "which thing" (saith our Lord) "I hate."[3] The Church in Thyatira "suffered that woman Jezebel" (some abominable heresy so styled from King Ahab's idolatrous queen) "to teach and seduce the servants of Christ, to commit fornication;"—they who had this doctrine are said to have "known the depths of Satan."[4] The Church in "Sardis lived, but was spiritually dead; the things which remained in her were ready to die; her works were not found perfect before God; she had but a few names" (in her) "which had not defiled their garments"[5]—*i.e.*, returned to their former pollutions

---

[1] Rev. ii, 5.   [2] *Ibid.* 4.   [3] *Ibid.* 14, 15.
[4] *Ibid.* 20, 24.   [5] *Ibid.* iii, 1, 2, 4.

after their regeneration. Lastly, the Church of the "Laodiceans was lukewarm, neither cold nor hot, indifferent to the truth, and therefore nigh unto rejection. She said she was rich" (*i.e.*, spiritually so) "and increased with goods, and had need of nothing; and knew not that she was almost reduced to her natural state again—was wretched, and miserable, and poor, and blind, and naked."[1] Such was the state of five of the seven Churches as early as in Domitian's reign;[2] and a very cursory perusal of the ecclesiastical historians will satisfy us, that they and the rest were not in a better way, after the conversion of the Roman empire. They were divided and torn asunder by innumerable heresies; and, to mention but one (under which all the rest may perhaps be finally reduced),[3] the impious doctrines

---

[1] Rev. iii, 15-17. [2] A.D. 95.

[3] For he that denies the divinity of Christ, denies all the merit and benefits of what he has done, or suffered, or can do for us—of his perfect obedience, sufferings, atonement, death, resurrection, and intercession. And he that denies the divinity of the Holy Spirit, denies the application of all that merit and those benefits to be redeemed—the inspiration, authority, and spirituality of his holy word—his divine presence in the blessed sacraments—his operation upon the souls of believers—and their spiritual union under one head: and so, in a word denies the whole of the covenant of grace, or restoration of lost mankind, by Jesus Christ—all the wisdom, and righteousness, and sanctification, and redemption, that God the Father hath given us, in and through God the Son, by God the Holy Ghost. So fruitful a parent of sin and sorrow, so plainly destructive of all the faith, hope, and love, that the mercy of our redeeming God

of Arius (of which the second Christian emperor

---

has shed abroad in the heart of fallen man, is the abominable, however fashionable, doctrine of Unitarianism! The Anti-Trinitarians will, I hope, take this matter seriously into consideration; and as they do not openly as yet, that I have heard, profess themselves to be Mahometans, it may be a useful hint to inform them here, that this their favourite opinion is the very essence of the Koran (the joint work, as well as the language in which it is written, *i.e.*, the modern Arabic, of an apostate Jew or Jews, and an excommunicated Nestorian monk), where they will read, amongst innumerable other instances of the same kind, the two following very remarkable ones—" Surely God will not pardon the giving him an equal, but will pardon any other sin, except that, to whom he pleaseth; and whoso giveth a companion unto God, hath devised a great wickedness." Chap. iv, called "the Chapter of Women." And again in the same chapter —" Believe therefore in God and his Apostles, and say not, there are three Gods (meaning three Persons, for the Christians deny three Gods, as well as the Mahometans) forbear this; it shall be better for you. God is but one God (meaning but one Person in the Godhead, as it follows) far be it from him, that he should have a Son." Sale's *Translation*, page 67, 81. To which I only beg leave to add, as a Christian, that then we have no eternal life—for the divine scriptures declare, " This life is in his Son." 1 John v, 11. And again more largely and emphatically, by a truly inspired messenger, St. John the Baptist—" He that believeth on the Son hath everlasting life; and he that believeth not the Son shall not see life, but the wrath of God abideth on him." John iii, 36. And let the Unitarian Deist remove it how he can, yea rather, let him apply for pardon in time through the divine merits of the God-man; and I pray the God of all mercy to the penitent, that his sin may be forgiven him, and his prayer find acceptance in the day of his trouble!

Constantius, and all the Gothic emperors afterwards were favourers) spread over the empire in a few years, were always its great reproach, and in the end its destruction: This was "denying the only Lord God and our Lord Jesus Christ,"[1] denying his divinity. Wherefore it pleased God at length to visit it for such repeated provocations. At a time when the emperor Heraclius (who was himself an heretic) was engaged in disputes, and by these means inattentive to the affairs of government, he suffered that vile imposter Mahomet to rise: had the emperor and his council been employed in the defence of the faith, it is likely, he either would not have risen, or the event have been different; but as it was, he and his successors extended their conquests with amazing rapidity; the sins of the empire made their victories easy; as the measure of them was not yet full, they indeed were to scourge it but in part; the final overthrow of it, with the reduction of Constantinople, was reserved for another Mahomet,[2] a fatal name indeed to Christianity! whose kingdom has been ever since the abomination of desolation to Christendom, as the Roman power was to Judea; and hangs now, like a heavy cloud, over the western empire, designed perhaps to break upon it too, when its infidelity is completed—for the throne of Mahomet is not supported for no end, and we have some reason to fear it is supported for this.

---

[1] Jude — 4.   [2] Mahomet II, emperor of the Turks.

Such awakening truths as these will surely lead us to reflect in what situation we ourselves stand towards God. The Churches, whose desolation you have heard, were once more flourishing than ours; they were fair primitive Churches; but like the numberless other glorious Churches in Asia and Africa, they are no more; their infidelity has long since turned them into a dark spiritual wilderness. Because they deserted their God, the Lord that bought them, he that had so loved them, forsook them: till they finally deserted him and his spiritual things, he forsook them not, but invited them with every overture of his mercy, and visited them with every chastisement of his love. But though space was given them to repent, they repented not. Wherefore their glory departed from them, as he had departed from Israel before, for the same reason; and left them too a dry, parched, barren desert, as he found them—no longer blessed with his all-cheering influences, and thence devoid of faith and all its amiable fruits—but dry, parched, and barren, exposed to wrath unexpiated only, unenlightened with the light of life, and unrefreshed with the dew of heaven! And as if the nature of their offence was intended to be set forth in the kind of their punishment, their desolation was wrought by the sword of a people,[1] whose religion is professed Unitarianism, and whose very hopes here, and supposed enjoyments

---

[1] The Mahometans.

hereafter, are as openly professed sensuality. Now great and manifold have been his mercies to this Church and nation; and there cannot be a fitter time to consider what effect they have had, than now we are met together to return public thanks for one of the greatest. Such the deliverance he vouchsafed us as upon this day ought to be esteemed, and such it will be esteemed by all, who will give attention to the troubles and miseries from which we were delivered. God was pleased, for the transgressions of our fathers, to permit a lawless, headstrong, enthusiastical faction to grow up in the heart of this kingdom, till it became at length too powerful to be subdued, even by force. The character of these malcontents very nearly resembles that of the abominable hereticks described by our Apostle, and St. Peter, in his second epistle. They did not indeed deny the Lord Jesus with their lips; they were too artful to do this; that blessed name was hardly ever out of their mouths; but by their works they denied him, and we are commanded to judge of them by their fruits. Some other parts of the character answer exactly in terms—they were "Murmurers, complainers, walking after their own lusts;"[1] "presumptuous, self-willed;"[2] "while they promised liberty, they themselves were the servants of corruption;"[3] they "despised dominion, and were not afraid to speak evil of dignities."[4] Thus qualified

---

[1] Jude—16.   [2] 2 Pet. ii, 10.   [3] *Ibib.* 19.   [4] Jude—8.

for any desperate undertaking, they set forward upon their intended reformation in Church and State; which, as indisputably appears from the treaties of Uxbridge and Newport, was not to rectify any abuses that might have crept into either, but utterly to abolish the then present form of government in both, and set up, in the stead of it, a general plan of independency, wherein their enthusiasm and ambition might safely riot at the expense of the public, without the least check or controul from any lawful authority. Reformation, however right and necessary in itself, under proper restrictions, has in all ages been the plea made use of by designing men, to recommend dangerous innovations; and whether the lately proposed emendations of our most excellent Liturgy did not proceed from the same spirit, now more gentle and candid, because it is not opposed, may, if the scheme should hereafter be revived, deserve your consideration. But at the time we are speaking of, this spirit was more daring. It petitioned for redress of grievances at the head of an army, and esteemed every thing a grievance that stood in the way of its favourite project. We cannot better finish the character of these men, than by shewing the manifest contrast there is, between what they pretended to be, and what they really were. As servants of the meek and merciful Jesus, they were high-minded and implacable; as his ser-

---

[1] 2 Pet. ii, 10.

vants, who " went about doing good," whithersoever they went, they spread devastation, exercising all kinds of rapine and violence ; as He came to save men's lives, they thought it their duty to destroy them ; as his subjects by whom kings reign, they were for extirpating monarchy, and blasphemously pleaded his commission so to do. But the event bore undeniable testimony to their principles:[1] notwithstanding all possible endeavours for a reconciliation, and more than legal concessions on the part of the crown, they proceeded to the most unheard of and execrable parricide, the public execution of one of the best men that ever sat on a throne, to the almost utter " desolation of two of these kingdoms, and the exceeding defacing and deforming the third."[2] Now, when both Church and State were thus deeply wounded, and there appeared but little hopes of the recovery of either, God was pleased

---

[1] The faithful Christian is the only faithful subject. The murder of kings, however justified upon the pretended principles of natural religion, ever has been, and ever must be, held abominable upon Christian principles. As in this one instance, among many, wherein the pretended principles of natural religion are expressly contrary to divine revelation, and therefore can never be a foundation for it to stand upon, I could not help taking notice of it, upon this occasion. Christian princes may herein see, which of their subjects are the loyalists, the Christians or the Deists, upon the allegiance of which, they may in all cases most securely depend. He, who is a traitor to Christ, cannot be faithful to his king.

[2] Lord Clarendon's *Hist. of the Rebellion.*

in a most extraordinary manner to heal all these wounds by his great mercy vouchsafed to us as upon this day,—" by restoring to us and his own just and undoubted rights, our then most gracious sovereign lord, king Charles II, thereby restoring also unto us the public and free profession of his true religion and worship, with our former peace and prosperity."[1] When we consider the remarkable steps by which this our deliverance was brought about, the unanimity of this at other times divided people to promote it, the seeming insufficiency of the means, and yet the amazing and almost incredible expedition with which the end was accomplished, we cannot but discern, and ought therefore to acknowledge, that " It was not our own arm that saved us, but his right-hand, and his arm, and the light of his countenance, because he had a favour unto us."[2] Such was the deliverance for which we are here met together to praise him; and now will be the proper time to enquire whether we have preserved a just and grateful sense of his mercies; for to apply to ourselves the emphatical words of Ezra, when he saw his people, just delivered from the Babylonish captivity, returning to their former abominations— "After all that is come upon us" (said he) "for our evil deeds and for our great trespass, seeing that thou our God hast punished us less than our iniqui-

---

[1] Second Collect in the service appointed for the day.
[2] Ps. xliv, 3.

ties deserve, and hast given us such deliverance as this; should we again break thy commandments, and join in affinity with the people of these abominations, wouldst not thou be angry with us, till thou hadst consumed us, so that there should be no remnant or escaping?"[1] And here it must be acknowledged, that the impression, made by the divine goodness upon the hearts of this people, was not so lasting as might reasonably have been expected. Being now again at ease, and in the full enjoyment of all kind of prosperity, like Jeshurun of old, "They waxed fat and kicked, they waxed fat, they grew thick, they were covered with fatness—then they forsook God which made them, and lightly esteemed the rock of their salvation."[2] Through a just abhorrence of fanatical hypocrisy, they ran headlong (as men are too apt to do) into the opposite extreme; as the enthusiastical party had "turned religion into rebellion," the succeeding politicians seem too much to have excluded it; and thereby very fatally gave encouragement to that diabolical scheme of natural Independency,[3] which affects the title of Deism, (though one inspired writer expressly declares, that

---

[1] Ez. ix, 13, 14.   [2] Moses's Song, Deut. xxxii, 15.
[3] Independency, arising out of pride and self-sufficiency, was the devil's crime; and the principles and practices, which threw him down from heaven, can never carry man to heaven: let all therefore, that hope to see the glory, from which he fell, beware of such principles and practices: the self-justifiers of the present age have great need of this caution.

"Whosoever denieth the Son, the same hath not the Father;"[1] and another, that they who are without Christ are without God, ἄθεοι[2]), which, as it falls in with the appetites of corrupt nature, and therefore cannot fail to recommend itself to men of lively parts and unmortified tempers, has ever since been gaining strength, and (as has been lately observed by an honest and able defender[3] of the "faith once delivered to the saints") "committed strange havock in this our clean and well-dressed vineyard, threatening not only the fences, but the very roots and productions of it."

It is time then for the watchmen to warn the people of their danger, and use the day of grace for their salvation and their own. What I have farther to offer upon this subject, I will now,

III. Lastly, collect into a few short reflections upon the whole, wherein it will appear, what qualifications are requisite on our part, for the religious celebration of this day's solemnity.

The impartiality of God's proceedings with mankind leaves impenitent infidelity, wherever it is found, no hope to escape; and the Apostle's argument, drawn from his dealings with Israel, now verified by sad experience, comes down to these our

---

[1] 1 John ii, 23.   [2] Eph. ii, 12.

[3] The truly learned and worthy Dr. Hodges, provost of Oriel College in Oxford, in his *Elihu, or an Inquiry into the Principal Scope and Design of the Book of Job.* Page 34. Quarto edition.

times with redoubled force. "Because of unbelief" (says he) "they were broken off, and thou standest by faith; be not high-minded, but fear; for if God spared not the natural branches, take heed lest he spare not thee. Behold therefore the goodness and severity of God, on them which fell, severity, but towards thee goodness, if thou continue in his goodness—otherwise thou also shalt be cut off."[1] He has long called us to repentance by his usual methods, and if, now his judgments are amongst us, we will not learn righteousness, our final visitation must be in vengeance: God forbid, that it should be so! and let it be our sincere endeavour, as far as we are able, to prevent it. This every one may do in some degree, by thinking upon his ways, by considering whether he hath contributed to obscure the light of the gospel in these kingdoms; and if he hath, to intreat God, while it is to-day, for his part of the transgression. But if his conscience condemn him not in this respect, he will yet do much by perseverance. Let him provoke the indifference of others by his zeal for the glory of God; let him publicly confess his master before men, "Esteeming the reproach of Christ greater riches than all the treasures of" the Egypt of "this world;" let him hold the doctrines of our most holy faith pure and uncorrupt; and if the primitive discipline is not restored by authority, "which our Church acknowledges is much to be

---

[1] Rom. xi, 20, etc.

wished," and, as the Lord has invested her with full power to maintain it, will most undoubtedly be required of her—let him revive it, as he shall have opportunity, by exercising it upon himself, and in the family, or other society, over which God hath placed, or shall place him.

But all this, and much more, will be required of the shepherds, in the present exigence. Let us, according to the solemn charge we have received " Before God and the Lord Jesus Christ, who shall judge the quick and the dead at his appearing and his kingdom, preach the word, be instant in season and out of season, reprove, rebuke, exhort with all long-suffering and doctrine; watch in all things, endure afflictions, do the work of evangelists, make full proof of our ministry."[1] Let us take example from the shepherds, as our flocks are commanded to do from the people of Israel: that we may not share in their punishment, let us have no share in their guilt, which the Lord thus layeth to their charge by the mouth of his prophet—" Son of man, prophecy against the shepherds of Israel, prophecy, and say unto them, thus saith the Lord God unto the shepherds—Wo be to the shepherds of Israel that do feed themselves; ye eat the fat, and ye cloath you with the wool, ye kill them that are fed, but ye feed not the flock—the diseased have ye not strengthened, neither have ye healed that which was

---

[1] 2 Tim. iv, 1, 2, 5.

sick, neither have ye brought again that which was driven away, neither have ye sought that which was lost—but with force and with cruelty have ye ruled them: and they were scattered because there was no shepherd, and they became meat to all the beasts of the field, when they were scattered."[1] Our duty particularly in warning the people of their danger, and, for our comfort, our full discharge too, when we have done our duty in this respect, are clearly set forth by the same prophet, in the preceding chapter, under a very exact and beautiful allusion, that of a watchman, set to give a city the alarm upon the approach of an enemy: "So thou, O son of man" (saith the Lord) "I have set thee a watchman to the house of Israel—therefore thou shalt hear the word at my mouth, and warn them from me. When I say unto the wicked, O wicked man, thou shalt surely die, if thou dost not speak to warn the wicked from his way, that wicked man shall die in his iniquity, but his blood will I require at thine hand: nevertheless, if thou warn the wicked of his way, to turn from it, if he do not turn from his way, he shall die in his iniquity, but thou hast delivered thy soul."[2]

Lastly, our chief dependence (under God) must be upon places of education, and may the divine Spirit engrave it in the memories of all who are intrusted with it in this place! More than ordinary

---

[1] Ezek. xxxiv, 1, etc.   [2] Ezek. xxxiii, 7, etc.

care should now be taken with the rising generation, to warn their hearts betimes with a deep and grateful sense of God's mercies, and enrich their understandings with the all-sufficient knowledge of his word; that the teachers, who go out from us, at least, may be both faithful and able stewards of his manifold grace. If the fountains themselves be corrupted, the streams, they send out to water the land, will be so of course, and the plants thereof will generally thrive or perish, according as they are watered.

To conclude.—Let us all then, in our several stations, and each of us according to his ability, strive to recover what is diminished of the dignity of the Church of England. Without such sentiments, such resolutions as these, I know not how we can celebrate this day as we ought to do. We may rejoice upon it indeed, without these qualifications, but we cannot, without them, keep it holy; we may observe it as a festival, but we cannot as a religious one: for how shall we praise God for blessings, which we neglect and despise? How pray for their continuance, when we will do nothing to perpetuate them? But with the above qualifications, we may approach the throne of grace, and humbly hope for success in our labours: at least, if the sins of the many should wax so strong, as to render our best endeavours with regard to the public welfare ineffectual, be entitled ourselves to God's mercies in Christ, both here and hereafter.

Now to God the Father, who was pleased to accept of a satisfaction for our sins ; to God the Son, who was pleased to make that satisfaction with his own blood to God the Father; and to God the Holy Ghost, who is pleased to sanctify all that are accepted of God the Father in God the Son ; to the most righteous, merciful and loving, eternal and adorable Trinity in Unity, be glory in the Church militant and triumphant, on earth and in heaven, for ever. Amen !

AARON'S INTERCESSION

AND

KORAH'S REBELLION CONSIDERED.

A

SERMON

PREACHED BEFORE THE UNIVERSITY OF OXFORD;

NOW PRINTED,

WITH WHAT THE AUTHOR JUDGED SOME SEASONABLE ADDITIONS;

AND

HUMBLY RECOMMENDED, AT THIS TIME OF VISITATION, TO THE ATTENTION OF THE PUBLIC;

BY

GEO. WATSON,

PRESBYTER OF THE CHURCH OF ENGLAND.

OXFORD:

PRINTED AT THE THEATRE FOR SACK. PARKER, AND R. CLEMENTS, IN OXFORD; AND E. WITHERS, AT THE SEVEN STARS, NEAR TEMPLE BAR, LONDON.

Imprimatur,
GEO. HUDDESFORD,
Vice-Can. Oxon.

Feb. 25, 1756.

PREFACE.

No true member of the Church of England, and loyal subject of the king, will find any difficulty of assent to the following sheets. Objections must come from the opposite quarter; and from such as believe the Holy Scriptures, I am aware of but two: 1, that the evidence here produced being brought from a transaction under the law, may not be conclusive under the Gospel dispensation; and 2, that the argument bears too hard upon the dissenters in its consequences; or, as I have heard it more invidiously expressed, that "I send all the dissenters to Hell." To the first objection an answer is occasionally given in the course of the sermon; but as what is there remarked may have greater weight in this place, where I am writing professedly upon the subject, and prepare the way for a more favourable reception of the kind of evidence used in the sermon, I shall here collect it, with some few additions, into one point of view; and it is briefly as follows. St. Paul, in his Epistle to the Romans, affirms that "whatsoever things were written aforetime, were written for our learning,"[1]—where the Apostle's assertion is general, evidently involving in it all the Scriptures of the Old Testament. But what can we learn from them, unless they are applicable to all times, and we in particular apply them to our own times and to ourselves, in order to avoid whatever is displeasing to God, and to do his blessed will, as he hath commanded us? Thus applied, they are so many standing lessons of divine instruction, as they were designed; and such examples of what hath been of old, with God's own determination in every case, besides their typical use in prefiguring Christ to us, and the spiritual things of his heavenly kingdom, often work more powerfully upon the heart, to reduce it to obedience, than the most forcible precept. But though this general evidence were sufficient for our purpose, and we might safely rest the matter upon it, we shall do well to observe further the particular applications of this sort by our blessed Saviour and his apostles. "As it was in the days of Noe," saith our Lord, "so shall it be also in the days of the Son of Man: they did eat, they drank, they married wives, they were given in marriage, until the day that Noe entered into the ark, and the flood came and destroyed them all."[2] And again, in the verse following: "Likewise also as it was in the days of Lot, they did eat, they drank, they bought, they sold, they planted, they builded; but the same day that

---

[1] Rom. xv, 4.   [2] Luke xvii, 26, 27.

Lot went out of Sodom, it rained fire and brimstone from Heaven, and destroyed them all. Even thus shall it be in the day when the Son of Man is revealed."[1] And again, in the next verse but one, where he is warning his disciples not to return back, after their spiritual deliverance, to their former worldly-mindedness,—but eminently at the time of Jerusalem's desolation, much more towards the destruction of the world, he saith,—" Remember Lot's wife."[2] In like manner saith his Apostle St. James, in his exhortation to the saints of God to endure the fiery trial of their faith : " Take, my brethren, the Prophets who have spoken in the name of the Lord,[3] for an example of suffering, affliction, and of patience";[4] adding for their encouragement, " Ye have heard of the patience of Job, and have seen the end of the Lord, that the Lord is very pitiful and of tender mercy."[5] So St. Peter, in his second Epistle, charges the infidelity of the last days with respect to Christ's second coming, and the dissolution of the heavens and earth by fire, according to his divine revelation, upon men's wilful ignorance of his judgment of old, executed by an universal deluge of water : " For this," saith he, " they are willingly ignorant of, that by the word of God the heavens were

---

[1] Luke xvii, 28, 29, 30.   [2] *Ibid.* v. 32.
[3] See a glorious catalogue of them in the eleventh chapter of the epistle to the Hebrews, and read on to the end of the Apostle's inference, in the following chapter.
[4] James v, 10.   [5] *Ibid.* 11.

of old, and the earth standing out of the water; and in the water, whereby the world that then was, being overflowed with water, perished."[1] St. Paul, in his Epistle to the Corinthians, hath taught us to make the same use of the Old Testament. "Now these things" (the things that befel the carnal Israel, from their deliverance out of Egypt to their overthrow in the wilderness,—and other scriptures carry it on to their final desolation,—all these things), the Apostle saith, were our examples, "to the intent we should not lust after evil things, as they also lusted," etc.[2] The reader will be pleased to read the chapter from the first to the fourteenth verse. Lastly, St. Jude has, amongst other instances, applied the very history now before us to some rebellious and heretical separatists in the apostolical age; thereby authorizing, I think, the future application of it to men of like sentiments or manners in every succeeding age of the Church, even to the end of the world. "Wo unto them," saith the Apostle, "for they have gone in the way of Cain, and ran greedily after the error of Balaam for reward, and perished in the gainsaying of Core."[3] I cannot see any evasion of this authority, unless perhaps it should be artfully urged that St. Jude, as an inspired writer, could not err in his application; whereas we who have no such infallible direction, may incur the charge of presumption in doing the like. That we have no such extraordi-

---

[1] 2 Peter iii, 5, 6. [2] 1 Cor. x, 6, etc. [3] Jude 11.

nary gifts now, amongst which the discerning of spirits was one,[1] I shall most readily allow; but that we cannot, therefore, form a certain judgment of men from their words and works, I am bound to deny,—first, because my blessed Master hath commanded me to do it, saying,—"Wherefore, by their fruits ye shall know them";[2] and secondly, because it is evident that, upon the contrary supposition, we could neither apply many histories of the Old Testament, or prophecies of the New, to one end for which they were designed. To judge of the thoughts of men's hearts is one thing; to judge of their overt acts, compared with God's written Word, is another. How far our modern Dissenters resemble those hereticks condemned by St. Jude, the impartial, will, upon comparison, determine for himself. I shall only assist his enquiry with suggesting one material part of the character of the latter, as drawn by the inspired pen of the aforementioned Apostle, that they despised dominion, and spake evil of dignities;[3] from the full meaning of which divine text, as we ought not to exclude the civil power, so neither can any one, without open violence to the context, exclude the ecclesiastical.

And here I might reasonably take my leave, without answering the second objection at all; since, if the former difficulty is obviated, the latter can be of no force—no man being answerable for the conse-

---

[1] 1 Cor. xii, 10.   [2] Matth. vii, 20.   [3] Jude 8.

quences of a scripture rightly applied or interpreted: they, whom it concerns, are to look to that. But as I would willingly be all things to all men, in the Apostle's sense, for their satisfaction I shall do my endeavour to give it in the present case to all that are disposed to receive it; that no supposed uncharitable zeal on my part may afford occasion to such as seek occasion, to draw away any one ignorant and unstable soul, or keep back, if already drawn away, any one returning soul, from God's undoubted institutions. With this view I now proceed therefore to the second objection above-mentioned, which was, that the argument bears too hard upon the Dissenters in its consequences, or, as I have heard it more invidiously expressed, that "I send all the dissenters to hell." My answer to which shall begin with an appeal to what I have written. Can any man read the following discourse, and say this? or will he not rather acknowledge it to be the very reverse of my intention? If warning a sinner from the error of his way be the sending of him to hell, what, let me ask it in God's name, is brotherly love? Whether all our Dissenters have not departed from the institutions of God (and I would the same might not now be said of most of them with respect to doctrine in some point or other), must be determined by the divine Scriptures, the only rule of faith and obedience; but if they have, then have they dangerously erred, in setting up their wisdom against the wisdom of God, and the calling upon them to return by a timely repentance, especially in this distracted state of the Church, is the duty of every faithful watchman, and a most charitable work. Whatever men may think now of this matter, through long custom and indifference, this was the opinion of holy and devout men, whose spirits are now, I trust, with God, in the primitive and every succeeding age of the Christian Church. One in particular has expressed what I wished to say on the subject in so clear and unexceptionable a manner, that the reader will be better pleased to read what remains of my apology in his most judicious words. After having assigned prudential reasons (if human prudence were our guide in such matters) why the episcopal form of government, if it were not a divine and unalterable institution, should, for the sake of uniformity, have been long since abolished, he proceeds thus :—

"But if the apostolical or episcopal form was ordained by Christ, for the perpetual and unalterable polity of his Church, as all Christianity in all ages believed for fifteen hundred years ; then let all the clergy write for it, as their worthy author hath done, expecting the protection of their great Lord here, and their reward from him hereafter, when they must give an account of this stewardship, and the authority he hath committed to them, for the government of his people. It is their duty to teach their flocks this fundamental doctrine of Church-government, and those which depend upon it, let the consequences of them fall upon what persons or Churches soever; and therefore let them teach them, without fearing to be reproached as high-flyers and men of rigid principles who had no charity, but are for damning all but themselves. These are slanders and persecutions, which those who will preach the truths and commandments of God, must be content to bear from those who cannot endure sound principles, because they make themselves obnoxious to the consequences of them; and then say, that they who preach them preach damnation to the greatest part of mankind, and to Christians as good as themselves. But I would ask those who are wont to talk after this loose manner, if I must not preach up the being and providence of God, because Atheists and Epicureans, who now are no small number, involve themselves in the consequences of a doctrine, which concludes them all under damning unbelief? Must I not assert the authority of the scripture, and the certainty of revealed religion, because it falls heavy upon the vast number of deists and sceptics among us, and puts them all in a state of damnation? Must I not preach up the union of the divine and human nature in the person of Christ, because the consequences of it are severe upon so many Arians, Socinians, and other Unitarians? Or, not to mention the moral doctrines of Christianity, must I not preach up the perpetual institution of the Lord's day, or of baptism, and the Lord's supper, because so many neglect, or despise, and reject the use of them, to their own destruction? In like manner let me ask these men, if the clergy must not preach up the episcopal form of Church-government as a perpetual ordinance of Christ, and the necessity of an episcopal mission and ministry, without respect to persons or Churches, be they never so many, which have rejected the divine institution, and still wilfully continue in the want of it, and thereby involve themselves in consequences which too many learned and worthy men, under the pretence of charity, have too much endeavoured to palliate, and soften, or evade for them; whereas it is much greater and truer charity to let those consequences fall in their full weight upon them, that they may see their error, and the danger of it by those consequences, and be thereupon effectually moved to reunite themselves to the Catholic Church, from whose doctrines they have departed in everything that relates to it as a society of Christ's framing,[1] and thereby brought

---

[1] Ignorance or disregard of this essential part of the constitution of a Church is, and ever has been, one grand cause of dissension. And as this mistake seems universally to obtain amongst Dissenters of all kinds, it will be of use to some readers, to add a short note upon what this judicious author has observed. A Church, then, is not only a number of people agreeing in the same articles of faith (although such unity of belief be an essential constituent of a Church), but it is also a society holding one visible communion under the same divinely-instituted government—or, as this worthy author expresses it, it is a society of Christ's framing. Opposite altars are like opposite thrones; different governments cannot make one society; a Church, as

their call and mission into question, giving as good and learned men as any are in the world occasion to doubt of their mission, whether it is valid or no; and by consequence, whether their ministers are God's ministers and messengers, such ministers as the archbishop (viz., Cranmer) speaks of in his sermon (on the power of the keys, which the reader will find at

---

well as a kingdom, divided against itself, must in the end be dissolved. St. Augustine has entered into this matter with his usual discernment. In one place, speaking to the Donatists, he says—"Ye are with us in baptism, in the creed, in all the other holy rites of our Lord's institution. But in the spirit of unity and bond of peace, finally, in the Catholic Church itself, ye are not with us."—Epist. xciii, p. 230, sect. 46. Edit. Benedict. And again, in another place, —" In many things they were with me. Both of us held baptism; in that they were with me. We kept the feasts of the martyrs; herein they were with me. We were constant at the anniversary of Easter; herein they were with me. But they were not altogether with me. In schism they were not with me, in heresy they were not with me. In many things they were with me, in some few things they were not with me. But by reason of the few things in which they are not with me, the many things in which they are with me do not profit them."—Enarratio in Ps. liv, tom. iv, p. 512. "Therefore," as the holy apostolic bishop and blessed martyr Ignatius exhorteth the Church in Philadelphia, " earnestly endeavour to partake of the same eucharist. For (there is) one flesh of our Lord Jesus Christ and one cup for the uniting of his blood. One altar, as (there is) one bishop (saith he) with the presbytery (*i.e.*, the priests) and deacons, my fellow servants; that whatsoever ye do, ye may do it accordingly to (the institution of) God."—Sect. iv.

the twenty-fifth page of his excellent preface), who have the true sacerdotal mission and authority from God, to minister his word and sacraments to the people in Christ's place, and the acts of whose ministry are as valid, as if Christ himself should minister unto them; as being made so by the same consecration, orders and unction, by which bishops and priests were made at the beginning, and are to be made God's ministers by his appointment, unto the end of the world? It grieves me always, when I consider to what difficulty the ministers of the Presbyterian Churches abroad have been put, to answer the questions about their mission; and what shifts and evasions their defenders among us have also been put to in their attempts to defend it. And therefore I must say it again, the greatest and truest charity to the reformed Churches, and the whole reformation, is to exhort them to take the same mission that we have retained, as the only true and indisputable mission of the holy Catholic Church. I think the nature of christian charity obliges us, upon Catholic principles, to write them up to our Church, and not, as the manner of some hath been, to write our Church down to them: and whoever would write such a parænesis (*i.e.*, exhortation), to them in the common language and christian spirit of meekness, I think he would do a most charitable work, for which, if they did not think themselves obliged to him, God would certainly reward him, and all good men would praise him for ever. What

I have said here I call God to witness, I speak not out of ill-will, but out of pure love and good-will, for the foreign reformed Protestants, for whose preservation, if I can judge of myself, I could lay down my life; and of whom I say with my whole heart, as St. Paul said to king Agrippa, I would to God, for his Church's sake, that they were not only almost but altogether as we of the Church of England are."

Thus far this great and useful light of the Church of England, Dr. Geo. Hickes,[1] in the forty-eighth and following pages of his preface to the divine right of episcopacy asserted, which together with the excellent book to which it is prefixed, I most earnestly recommend to the attentive perusal of the pious believer, as containing the best information I have met with for general use, in this important enquiry—wherein is proved by an induction of particulars faithfully collected from the word of God, and writings of the primitive fathers, that episcopacy is of divine and apostolical institution, and that it was the government of the Christian Church during the three first ages of it, and was designed to be perpetual in it to the end of the world—with an account of the distinction of the three orders of bishop, priest, and deacon, to reconcile the dissenting parties to that form of Church-government.

I have only now to add a brief exhortation to those into whose hands these sheets may come, that laying

---

[1] *Vide* editor's note at the end of this preface.

aside every prejudice of their own, and giving no heed to the specious suggestions of men of latitudinarian principles, they will, with due reference and humility of soul, take their instruction from God; since to be wise above what is written, whether it be in matters of doctrine or institution, is to throw up the reins to inordinate affection, and multiply error without end. I intreat them to consider well the consequences this has already produced—how far their plea of prejudice of education, which is the being led by authority, will be admitted in a country where the holy scriptures are, or may be, in every man's hand—and whether anything they have heard or may hear, can be esteemed a safe counterbalance to the infallible direction of Almighty God, and the universal practice of his Church, grounded thereupon, for the space of fifteen hundred years. These reflections, duly weighed, with the careful reading of the book and preface above recommended, will, I trust, be sufficient for the conviction of every sincere well-meaning dissenter: and I most devoutly beseech our Lord Jesus, that great shepherd of the sheep,[1] to hasten the return of such, as wander thus unwittingly, into the fold of his Church. From the rest, whom the God of this world hath blinded, who view every object placed before them through the medium of present gratification, I have no other treatment to expect than better writers and much

---

[1] Heb. xiii, 20.

better men have experienced before me : bearing in mind my Saviour's words : "The disciple is not above (his) master, nor the servant above his Lord : it is enough for the disciple that he be as his Master, and the servant as his Lord,"[1]—who, though it was testified of him before he came, " grace is poured into thy lips,"[2] and who accordingly when he came, "spake as never man spake"[3]—yea, " who loved as never man loved," and obeyed as never man obeyed, (such is the base ingratitude of this sinful world !)— was only nailed to the cross for it.

---

[1] Matth. x, 24, 25.   [2] Ps. xlv, 2.   [3] John vii, 46.

[Dr. George Hickes was made a prebendary of Worcester in 1680, and in August, 1683, was promoted to the deanery. At the revolution in 1688 he refused to take the oaths of allegiance, and fell under suspension in 1689, and was deposed the following February of his preferment, against which he protested, and affixed his claim on the great entrance into the choir. Expecting on this account the resentment of the government, he privately withdrew to London, where he concealed himself for many years, until Lord Somers, then Chancellor, procured an act of council by which the Attorney-General was ordered to cause a *non prosequi* to stay proceedings against him. He afterwards went to France with the list of deprived clergy, to confer with King James about the matter, and returned to England in February, 1694, and on the eve of St. Matthias he was consecrated suffragan bishop of Thetford. Being thus spiritually a bishop, he exercised his duties by ordaining priests and deacons, but he became so obnoxious to the government that his personal safety was often greatly endangered. He was frequently under the necessity of keeping himself closely concealed and going in disguise, and it is related by the continuator of the life of Dr. Kettlewell, that once meeting Dr. Hickes, he was surprised at observing him in a military dress and passing for a captain or a major. He died in 1715. He was a man of unusual learning, well versed in the northern languages. In 1705 he published one of the most extraordinary Herculean labours ever attempted, entitled "Linguarum vett. Septentrionalium Thesaurus grammatico-criticus et archæologicus." Oxon., 1703-5. Fol. 3 vols. With a splendid portrait of the Doctor. On his becoming Dean of Worcester he commenced a long and endearing friendship with Dr. Hopkins, a prebendary, whose life the dean afterwards prefixed to a volume of Dr. Hopkins' sermons. It is a piece of biography not so well known as it deserves, in which the dean states the obligations he was under to the worthy prebendary, in bringing about many reforms of abuses which they found existing in the chapter.]—NOTE BY EDITOR.

AARON'S INTERCESSION

AND

KORAH'S REBELLION CONSIDERED.

A SERMON.

NUMBERS xvi, 47, 48.

And Aaron took as Moses commanded, and ran into the midst of the congregation, and behold the plague was begun among the people; and he put on incense, and made an atonement for the people—and he stood between the dead and the living, and the plague was stayed.

THESE words contain a most awful and interesting description. All the circumstances of it are so striking, so full of terror on the one hand, and of consolation on the other—the colouring so strong—the distress so exquisite—and the deliverance so extraordinary, so unexpected, so unmerited—that the bare recital of it cannot but sensibly affect you, and move every compassionate heart that has any feeling for others. Much more will it, when you consider the design of the history, how nearly yourselves are concerned in it. For we have divine authority to affirm that "the things which happened to Israel of old," under that figurative dispensation, " happened unto them for examples to us, the Christian Church in the latter days; and that they are written for our admonition, upon whom the ends of the world are come."[1] Yea, that all things, "whatsoever were written aforetime, in the Scriptures of the Old Testament, were written for our learning—and were written for this end, that we, through patience and comfort of the Scriptures, might have hope."[2] The scripture before us therefore was written for this end; and if it shall now raise or confirm this hope in any that are here present, it shall have accomplished in every such person, the end for which it was written. I shall endeavour, by the blessing of God, to place it in such a point of view, as to produce this blessed effect in the hearts of many that hear me. I shall for this purpose,

I. Lay before you the historical relation, the occasion of Aaron's interposition, and the consequence of it.

II. Show the merciful design, in recording it, what it was intended to represent.

III. The farther instruction that arises from the history thus illustrated and explained. I am

I. To lay before you the historical relation, the occasion of Aaron's interposition, and the consequence of it.

The occasion was this:—Korah, Dathan and Abiram, with certain others they had seduced, had rebelled against Moses and Aaron, presumptuously

---

[1] 1 Cor. x, 11.   [2] Rom. xv, 4.

claiming to themselves, and intruding into those high and separated offices, which no man could take upon himself without God's appointment, and had received their punishment, a punishment as extraordinary as the offence! For the Lord made a new thing, as his servant Moses had foretold, "and it came to pass, as he had made an end of speaking, &c., that the ground clave asunder that was under them, and the earth opened her mouth, and swallowed them up, and their houses and all the men that (appertained) unto Korah, and all their goods, they and all that (appertained) to them, went down alive into the pit, and the earth closed upon them, and they perished from among the congregation. And there came out a fire from the Lord, and consumed the two hundred and fifty men that offered incense."[1] So miraculous a manifestation of God's displeasure would, one should have thought, have silenced the multitude, and terrified the most hardened of them into obedience. They fled indeed "at the cry of them that suffered, for they said lest the earth swallow us up also."[2] But as soon as the danger was over, they discovered the real sentiments of their corrupted hearts. All reverence laid aside, they go in a tumultuous and insolent manner to their leaders, requiring at their hands the blood of Korah and his followers. "On the morrow all the congregation of the children of Israel murmured against Moses and against Aaron, saying, ye

---

[1] Numbers xvi, 30, 31, 32, 33-35.   [2] Verse 34.

have killed the children of the Lord."[1] Thus, by standing up for these offenders, they shewed a secret approbation of their offence, and being partakers of their offence, they justly became also partakers of their destruction. The divine wrath therefore went out against them. "Get you up, said the Lord to Moses and Aaron, from among this congregation, that I may consume them in a moment."[2] A most dreadful pestilence ensued: and then it was, that Aaron did, as it is recorded of him in the text—" took a censor with fire from off the altar, and put on incense as Moses commanded, and ran into the midst of the congregation, and made an atonement for the people."[3] He exposed himself for their sake to the irresistible displeasure of his God, which had already swept away such numbers of them—stood in the mid way between the wrath and them, between the dead and the living—an action so full of faith and love, as to deserve the admiration of all ages; unexampled, except in the cases of Moses and David, who offered themselves in like circumstances to save their people; and never but once exceeded,—I mean by that great mediation, of which all these were types—as they well knew who interposed, or they would never have dared to interpose!

The consequence of this interposition was, that the plague was stayed. It stopped where Aaron

---

[1] Numbers xvi, 41.   [2] Numbers xvi, 45.
[3] Numbers xvi, 47.

stood; before him all were consumed, all behind him were saved—he "stood between the dead and the living." But was it for Aaron's sake, that God spared the remnant of his people? Had he any merit of his own, any superfluous righteousness that might be imputed to them? So far from it, that, however comparatively holy and faithful he was, yet was he a descendant of that Adam, of whose children it was testified, that "there is none that doeth good, no not one."[1] He, and every high priest, taken from among men, were necessarily heirs of the universal corruption, had their infirmities, as the Apostle argues, and were obliged to offer up sacrifice for their own sins, as well as those of the people.[2] Aaron therefore of himself could make no atonement for them; and without an atonement, the justice of God could not let them escape. To account for this wonderful deliverance then, we must carry on our thoughts farther, to some higher atonement, to a greater than Aaron, as we shall do by considering, as was proposed,

II. The merciful design in recording this history, what it was intended to represent.

And St. Paul, in his epistle to the Hebrews, has determined this point beyond all contradiction. He tells us, that the "law had a shadow of good things to come," of which Christ and his heavenly things

---

[1] Ps. liii, 1, 3; compare Rom. iii, 12.
[2] Heb. v, 1; vii, 27.

were the body;[1] that Aaron and every high priest were his representatives, who is our gracious intercessor and high priest for ever;[2] the holy of holies, and all Aaron did there before the cherubim of glory upon the mercy-seat, types or figures of heaven itself, and what our Lord did and does there in the presence of God for us;[3] and the blood he there offered once a year, emblematical of his blood, who offered himself once for all.[4] Taking it therefore for granted, since the Holy Ghost expressly affirms it, that Aaron represented our Lord at all times, I shall pass on to the true application of the history before us, and lay open the spiritual intention of it; whereby it will appear that this thing, as well as all others recorded of God's people, " happened unto them for an ensample, and is written," (is now left upon record in the bible), " for our admonition, upon whom the ends of the world," the latter days, those of the Messiah, " are come."[5]

We have here then described to us, under the most affecting images, the miserable and lost state of man after the fall; the terrible execution of divine justice on the one hand, and the gracious interposition of our Redeemer on the other, with the effects of both. We and all mankind are rebels by nature —in Adam all sinned[6]—all broke their allegiance to

---

[1] Ch. x, 1, 9, 10, 11, 12, 23, 24.   See also Coloss. ii, 17.
[2] Hebr. ix, 7, 8, 9, 10, 11, etc.
[3] Hebr. ix, 7, 24.
[4] Hebr. ix, 9, 12, 26.
[5] 1 Cor. x, 11.
[6] Rom. v, 12, 19.

their Creator and Sovereign, and went over to his and their enemy. Forfeiture of life and inheritance necessarily followed the transgression—in Adam all died[1]—died from God, from his spirit and glory, as well as became mortal in their bodies, were subjected to the sentence of the spiritual and eternal, as well as natural death; *i.e.*, our spirits were deprived by sin of all communication with God in this life,[2] as they, and our souls and bodies were to be of his glorious presence[3] in outer darkness[4] for ever[5]—being all doomed to be cast finally into the lake of fire,[6] which the Holy Ghost by St. John emphatically styles the "second death:"[7] in which complete sense of the word death therefore, as it respects the present, separate, and after state of the spirit, soul, and body, "death passed upon all men, for that all have sinned."[8] The unquenchable fire of divine wrath being thus kindled up against us, justice must ever after have taken place, without mercy, all have been involved in the common ruin, without distinction, without hope. But this was not the end for which the blessed Trinity created man. For God made not death—he created man to be immortal, and made him to be an image of his own eternity —through envy of the devil came death into the world, and "still, as at first, they" alone "that do

---

[1] Rom. v, 12, 14, 15, 17, 21 ; 1 Cor. xv, 22.
[2] Ephes. iv, 18.   [3] Matth. x, 28 ; 2 Thess. i, 9.
[4] Matth. xxii, 13.   [5] Rev. xiv, 11.
[6] Rev. xx, 14.   [7] *Ibid.* 14.   [8] Rom. v, 12.

hold of his side do find it."[1] For the covenant of works being broken by transgression, the covenant of grace, or Christianity, now immediately succeeded—the gracious remedy provided against sin and death, when they should be introduced into the works of God, the blessed means of eternal reconciliation, foreordained of the Persons in the Deity before the foundation of the world, that the sinner, who had no righteousness of his own to plead in arrest of God's righteous judgment, might, upon the new terms of this act of grace, again find acceptance and life through the divine satisfaction and imputed righteousness of our Lord Jesus Christ. In pursuance of which divine council, he, the second Person, the true Aaron, our everlasting high priest and representative, ran into the midst of God's people; as is indeed expressed in his title of mediator, which signifies a person who interposes between two parties at variance, to the end that he may reconcile them. Being made flesh in the fulness of time, he met the burning wrath in our stead,[2] and by virtue of his unchangeable purpose so to do, turned it aside from all believers, as well before he came as afterwards. In the particular of his sufferings indeed Aaron could not represent him; this the sacrifices, as far as was possible, were designed to represent; their blood was shed instead of the sinner's blood, the fire

---

[1] Author of the book of Wisdom i, 13; ii, 23, 24.
[2] Lam. i, 12; Isaiah liii, 5, 6.

consumed them instead of the offerer. But as Aaron with the offered incense made a typical atonement for the people, so did He a real by his merits, which that incense represented.[1] He stood, and stands now, between the dead and the living—those who, by opposing his method of saving them, will die in their sins, and those who, believing in him, though they were dead, yet shall live, who, living and believing in him, shall never die.[2] "And the plague is stayed." He paid the ransom for all mankind that will accept of it. Over such as do, the second death shall have no power. The fiery sword of offended justice cannot reach them; he was pierced through with it in their stead. "There is therefore now," as saith the Apostle, "no condemnation to them which are in Christ Jesus,"[3] who utterly renouncing the filthy rags of their own sinful righteousness,[4]—as all the righteousness fallen man can work, even under grace, must be, because he that works it is a sinner —every thing they can do towards their own justification, towards the payment of that infinite debt they have contracted, and are still contracting— humbly sue for his divine righteousness, who has paid it for them to the uttermost, the only meritorious and availing righteousness, the righteousness that is by faith;[5] who thus divesting themselves of their own merit, plead his only for acceptance—

---

[1] Rev. viii, 3. [2] John viii, 24. [3] Rom. viii, 1. [4] Isaiah lxiv, 6.
[5] See Rom. iii, 19, 20, 21, 23, 24, 25, 26.

acknowledge their spiritual nakedness, and seek his covering and protection. Such indeed as despise the riches of his mercy, and oppose him in the way of his salvation, rebel against the inward operations of his Holy Spirit, or the outward appointments of his word and sacraments. Such shall undoubtedly perish "in the gainsaying of Core," which are the words of the Apostle St. Jude;[1] and being spoken of the opposers in his days, with reference to the transaction before us, add a peculiar force and even inspired testimony to our application of this history; shewing it to be set forth as a "lesson of instruction for the sons of Korah," a standing monument of the wrath of God against every such audacious rebel, every antichristian blaspheming gainsayer, to the end of the world. To such "there remaineth no more sacrifice for sins, but a certain fearful looking for of judgment and fiery indignation, which shall devour the adversaries."[2] Such, having rejected the terms of grace and forgiveness, excluded themselves from all the benefits of Christ's mediation, must bear the whole weight of God's displeasure themselves; where there is no substitute, the soul that sinneth it must die; a dreadful consideration this; it is a fearful thing to fall into the hands of the living God, "for our God is a consuming fire."[3] The possibility of this, much more the certainty of it, is surely enough

---

[1] Rom. iii, 11.   [2] Hebr. x, 26, 27.
[3] *Ibid.* xii, 19, from Deut. iv, 24.

to determine every serious person to "fly for refuge, to lay hold upon the hope" (that is) "set before us."[1]

By this time you must all have observed, that something more was intended by the words I have been endeavouring to explain to you, than a bare relation of what the high priest of Israel did upon this extraordinary occasion, for the people of that nation only; and from what has been said you may easily collect the reason that Aaron's interposition on their behalf was so effectual. For if Aaron represented Christ in these circumstances, and the atonement he made for the remnant of Israel the great atonement our Lord was to make for the Israel of God, the true Church in all ages past and to come, then God had undoubtedly respect to that great atonement, and for his sake who was to make it, pardoned those for whom it was to be made. Thus is the whole transaction placed in its true light; the use we are to make of it set forth; and this Scripture shewn to be in particular, what St. Paul affirms of all Scripture in general, " profitable for instruction in righteousness,"[2] that is, the righteousness of Christ, imputed to us, or the doctrine of justification by his merits only.

You have now heard the particulars of this affecting history, with the end for which this thing happened to Israel, and is since recorded in holy writ; which was, to declare to them and us the only possi-

---

[1] Heb. vi, 18.   [2] Tim. iii. 16.

ble way of salvation, the inevitable ruin of all opposition to the truth and ordinances of Christ, and the sure deliverance that would always accompany his divine mediation. May grace be given to every one of you to consider the history in this light! that they, who see no redemption out of him, may receive this additional evidence of their hope; and they who do not as yet see it, may intreat him to open the blinded eyes of their understanding,[1] that they also, seeing it ere it is too late, may obtain the benefits of his atonement, and find a shelter therein from the storm that is one day to be poured out upon the world. The farther instruction I proposed,

III. To collect from the history, thus illustrated and explained, is partly deducible from the history itself, and partly from the spiritual exposition of it.

1. From the history itself we learn, 1. The necessity there is of an outward consecration to the priesthood, and that in the way of God's institution; 2. The subordination He himself has appointed amongst the persons so consecrated; and 3. The great duty of universal obedience to all lawful authority. Our numerous schismatics would do well to attend to the history in these points of view. It is a powerful argument to persuade such persons to lay aside their unreasonable prejudices, and what, I fear, is a more general obstacle, their less excusable worldly interests, since whoever hopes to make a part of the

---

[1] 2 Cor. iv, 4; Ephes. iv, 18.

Church in heaven must maintain the unity, which cannot be maintained without maintaining the government of it upon earth: Korah, Dathan, and Abiram, for breaking in upon these, perished from among the congregation.

Those who, with the Deists, oppose all divine institutions whatever, and that of ordination in particular, will here see the high sin and danger of assuming the sacred office without it; which is to throw down boundaries set up by God himself, and lay open what he has inclosed. Such will remember the fire that came out from the presence of the Lord, and consumed the two hundred and fifty men that offered incense. Pretences of equal or even superior holiness, we learn, will not be admitted. This was the plea of Korah and his associates,—(ye take) "too much upon you, seeing all the congregation are holy, every one of them, and the Lord is among them; wherefore then lift ye up yourselves above the congregation of the Lord?"[1] But this was false—for the Lord was against them, and shewed the most dreadful signs of his displeasure. His wrath waxed more than ordinarily hot against these self-commissioned holy ones, however qualified in their own conceit to approach him. And the case would have been the same, if they had been as holy as they pretended to be. For there is a sanctity of office as well as of life, an outward separation of particular persons for

---

[1] Numbers xvi, 3.

the ministration in holy things, as well as an inward one of all believers from the corruption of this evil world ; and whoever confounds this separation, or holiness of office, with the personal holiness of sanctification, in order to set aside the divine institution, is, according to God's own determination in this history, a sinner against his own soul. Want of personal holiness in our governors is at their peril, and a heavy account it will be, as disobedience and usurpation of their office is at our's.

2. They, who allow of no subordination in the ministry, will observe, that the grand conspirator was a Levite, whose office represented that of the deacons under the gospel dispensation. For such to disturb the peace within the sanctuary, through their avarice or ambition, is as ungodly, as for those who are not ordained thereunto to press into it from without. Such, 'tis to be hoped, will lend an ear to Moses, the inspired servant of God, who said unto Korah, &c. :—"Hear, I pray you, ye sons of Levi, (seemeth it but) a small thing unto you, that the God of Israel hath separated you from the congregation of Israel to bring you near to himself, to do the service of the tabernacle of the Lord, and to stand before the congregation to minister unto them ? And he hath brought thee near to him, and all thy brethren, the sons of Levi, with thee, and seek ye the priesthood also?"[1] That was not their appointment. But

---

[1] Numbers xvi. 8, 9, 10.

the rebellious Levite would brook no reproof; and as he still persisted in his demand, "the ground clave asunder that was under him, and he went down alive into the pit."[1]

If it should be doubted, as many upon their principles must doubt, who assume what is peculiar to the episcopal office, appointing others to the work of the ministry, sending them out un-ordained, or, which is the same, ordained as they speak, by themselves,—if such should doubt, whether the priest might not have done what the Levite perished for attempting, they will find a satisfactory answer, I should hope, in considering, that though every priest, duly consecrated, was a type of Christ, and all equally empowered under due regulation to preach the word of God, and administer his sacraments, yet the high priest had some peculiar offices, into which no man was to intrude; which, besides the typical respect they had to Christ himself, were undoubtedly a figure[2]

---

[1] Numbers xvi, 38.

[2] The apostolical father St. Clement, manifestly in allusion to this, speaketh in the following manner of the Christian ministry. "For to the high-priest his proper services are committed, and to the priests their proper place is appointed, and upon the Levites lays the charge of their proper ministries; the lay man is limited by laical precepts (*i.e.*, such as properly concern the lay man.) Let every one of you, brethren, give thanks to God in his proper order, living with a good conscience, and through a becoming reverence, not transgressing the prescribed rule of his ministry." 1 Epist. to the Corinthians, sect. xl, which, with the rest, particularly the six immediately following sections of

of the subordination after instituted in the christian Church, which was episcopal from the beginning; and that Nadab and Abihu, the sons of Aaron, the priests, for transgressing a divine institution, for offering strange fire before the Lord, which he commanded not, actually died the same death with the two hundred and fifty rebels in this history. "There went out a fire from the Lord, and devoured them, and they died before the Lord."[1] Their contempt and violation of divine ordinances was, we see, a capital offence. Rebellion in an officer is doubly sinful, and God forbid the officers of the great king should upon any pretence encourage it! No—let the stars of the earthly sanctuary be examples to all the rest, be particularly careful to keep that order they are to influence others to maintain. They will then shine most for his glory, who hath appointed their courses with unerring wisdom, and most for the benefit of his Church, which is best served in the

---

this ancient and most valuable epistle, I could wish the serious reader would attentively peruse, as a plain and irrefragable testimony of what is here aserted, of the highest merely-human authority—as coming from one, who not only conversed with, and was appointed a bishop by the apostles themselves, but whose name is moreover expressly declared to be " in the book of life." Philip. iv, 3. The English reader may read this, and the other genuine epistles of the apostolical fathers, S. Polycarp, S. Ignatius (whom I would particularly recommend on the subject of episcopacy), etc., in Archbishop Wake's *Translation*.

[1] Levit. x, 1, 2.

way He that loveth her best hath appointed. His Angels, that preserved their allegiance, now surround the throne of his glory ; but the angels which kept not their first estate, but left their own habitations, he hath reserved in everlasting chains under darkness, unto the judgment of the great day.[1] Even so his faithful ministers on earth, who abide in his ordinances, as well as truth, shall shine as the brightness of the firmament, and as the stars for ever and ever,[2] however differing, as they do in the material firmament, in the degrees of their glory; but for such disorderly ones as quit their station, the wandering stars, mentioned by the apostle, for such we know is reserved an end suitable to their lawless motions here, even the blackness of darkness out of the glorious system of the new creation, for ever.[3]

3. Indeed, the material heavens are continually teaching us the great lesson of obedience; and let every star in the spiritual firmament so do his father's will upon earth, reflect the light he receives, not as he thinks right, but as the sun of righteousness has directed. Obedience, growing out of faith, is one of the fairest fruits of regeneration, as it shows the stubborn soil of the natural ground to be broken and subdued by the spirit, the heart and its inordinate lusts to be brought in subjection to the law of God. Rebellion ever riseth up out of the bitter root of corruption. To despise dominion and speak evil of

---

[1] Jude — 5, 6.   [2] Dan. xii, 3.   [3] Jude — 5, 13.

dignities[1] was a mark of false teachers in the days of the apostles; as to be traitors, heady and high-minded, is of the perilous times in the last days,[2] which I the rather mention, as some, who insist most upon the inward experience of their sanctification, (however such experience, a joy in the Holy Ghost, when accompanied with the other evidences of sanctification, ought to be insisted upon,) do, at the same time, if we may judge of them by their fruits, shew a most unsanctified spirit, by setting themselves up and teaching others to rebel against their spiritual governors. But, my brethren, be not you carried about with every wind of doctrine, by the sleight of men, the cunning craftiness, whereby they lie in wait to deceive.[3] No man speaking by the spirit of God, can contradict what the spirit hath written; no one faithfully executing a divine commission, transgress a divine institution, which is, to set aside the same authority in one respect that he allows in another. You have an infallible rule to direct your judgment as well as practice in such cases. Now I beseech you, brethren, says the apostle, mark them which cause divisions and offences contrary to the doctrine which ye have learned, and avoid them; for they that are such serve not our Lord Jesus Christ, but their own belly, and by good words and fair speeches, deceive the hearts of the simple.[4] And

---

[1] Jude — 8.   [2] 2 Tim. iii, 1.   [3] Ephes. iv, 14.
[4] Rom. xvi, 17, 18.

lest such as are led away into schism, should esteem it a matter of indifference, or that this comprehensive history contains no instruction for them, they will recollect the destroying pestilence, as well as devouring pit, and consuming fire; that beside them that died about the matter of Korah, there died in the plague of people who justified the fact, fourteen thousand and seven hundred.[1] Wherefore as St. Augustin most excellently adviseth, seeing " the Church in this world consisteth of chaff and wheat, let no one try to drive out all the chaff until the time of winnowing. Let no one leave the threshing-floor before the time, lest, while peradventure he will not bear with sinners, being found without the threshing-floor, he should be picked up by the birds ere he can return into the barn."[2]

Lastly. As Korah, &c., rebelled against Moses, the vice-roy of God, as well as against Aaron his high-priest, against neither of whom it was lawful even so much as to speak evil,[3]—the factious and levelling spirits in civil governments may here read their condemnation: what our Lord, his holy prophets, and apostles taught by word and example, that the pit, fire, and pestilence in this history do most awfully proclaim. Let every soul be subject to the higher powers;[4]—whether it be to the king as supreme (to whom, therefore, every inferior magistrate, as being

---

[1] Numb. xvi, 49. [2] St. Aug. in Ps. xxv.
[3] Exod. xxii, 28; Acts xxiii, 5. [4] Rom. xiii, 1.

one of his people, must needs be subject, the same subordination being here discernible among the civil powers, as was above observed among the ecclesiastical for the two hundred-and-fifty rebels, whom the fire consumed, are styled princes of the assembly [1]), or unto governors (rulers of provinces, &c., but inclusively to all other duly-appointed magistrates and officers) that are sent by him (that have their commission from the king), for the punishment of evildoers, and for the praise of them that do well.[2] The reason is, there is no power but of God, the powers that be, the rulers established for the time being, are ordained of him. Whosoever, therefore, resisteth the power, resisteth the ordinance of God : herein lies the sin of resistance then, it is God whom such independents resist. Korah, &c., were gathered against Jehovah, saith Moses,[3] whosoever resisteth, resisteth the ordinance of God, saith St. Paul; and the end of such resistance is that invisible pit, and unquenchable fire, of which the pit and fire in this history were only figurative representations—for so it follows—and they that resist shall receive to themselves damnation.[4] This is a strange doctrine to bring to the ears of a licentious people; but it is the doctrine of the bible universally, and of this history in particular ; and if the hearts of any professing christianity are not yet prepared to admit it,

---

[1] Numb. xvi, 2.   [2] 1 Pet. ii, 13, 14.
[3] Numb. xvi, 11. [4] Rom. xiii, 2.

they must pray for grace and lowliness of spirit, for those are the requisite preparations. But whether they admit it or not, we should show our obedience in preaching it, that we handle not the word of God deceitfully, and that our gospel be not hindered, to which we should give occasion indeed, if, by confounding our spiritual freedom with civil licentiousness, we should use (our) liberty for a cloke of maliciousness, and not as the servants of God.[1] A rebellious christian is a most flagrant contradiction —what? Christ, the author of rebellion? No—away with it from the garden of the church into his kingdom to the world, who raised the first rebellion and heresy in heaven, and shall inspire the last upon earth. The primitive saints, whose example is of the highest authority next to those of our Lord, his holy prophets and apostles, who were so eminent for sanctity in every respect, were of all men the most obedient. They submitted themselves to their appointed governors, even as to him who appointed them, were obedient to those that had the spiritual rule over them, unto the severest discipline; were obedient to the civil power, unto the loss of all things, were obedient even unto death.

II. From the spiritual exposition of the history we infer, what the holy scriptures throughout expressly declare, that God does require a satisfaction for sin. This the enemies of the cross oppose, upon what

---

[1] 1 Pet. ii, 16.

principle is hard to say, except that, upon which the apostate angels opposed it, at the first revelation of it in heaven, pride, or self-sufficiency,[1] which desperately prefers everlasting ruin to salvation by the merits of another, even though the Saviour be God himself.[2] For that God is just, and that to require a satisfaction for sin is justice, that otherwise he

---

[1] 1 Tim. iii, 6.

[2] The reader will find incontestable proofs of our Lord's divinity in the following scriptures:—Gen. i, 1 (compared with John i, 3, 10; Col. i, 16; and Heb. i, 2, 3, 8, 10, etc.; iii, 4); xxvi, 3, 22; xvii, 1. Exod. iii, 4, 6, 7, 11, 13, 14, etc.; xix, 17, 18, 19, 20, etc. Ps. lxxx, 1, 3, 4, etc.; lxxxii, 8. (Compare John v, 22); Isaiah ix, 6; xxv, 9; Mal. iii, 2. (Compare Luke i, 76); Matth. xxviii, 19; Luke i, 78; John ii, 24, 25; iii, 31; v, 17; viii, 16, 19, 58; x, 30, 33; 1 Epist. v, 7, 20; Acts vii, 59; Rom. iv, 17; viii, 11; ix, 5; Ephes. v, 27; Coloss. ii, 9; 2 Cor. xiii, 14; 1 Tim. vi, 14, 15, 16. (Compare Revelations xvii, 14; xix, 16, 17); Titus ii, 10, 13; Hebrews i, 8 from Ps. xlv, 6; Rev. i, 8, 18; iv, 8, 9, 10, 11. (Compare Isaiah vi, 3); xi, 15. (Compare v, 17), and, not to multiply instances here without number, in every place where the divine incommunicable name Jehovah—which is generally rendered Lord, and printed in capitals in English bibles—the divine attributes, all-sufficient, all-wise, all-mighty, etc.—the divine covenant, or relative titles, divine acts and offices,—as God (אלהים, in the plural number), Son, Lord, light, glory, etc., creator, upholder of all things, redeemer, intercessor, and judge, etc., are ascribed to him; as one or more of them are on all his appearances before and under the law, as well as at and after his manifestation in the flesh, *i. e.*, in a word, from the first chapter of the book of Genesis to the last of the Revelations.

were not just, they cannot rationally deny. But notwithstanding the self destroying opposition of these sinful men, the truth stands as unshaken as its everlasting Author; it was said, and it is written,—" In the day thou eatest thereof thou shalt surely die."[1] Which, with regard to its effect on our first parents, as a gracious provision had been made for the restoration of fallen man, and God, when he said this, knew they would thankfully accept of it, is to be understood of the spiritual and natural death only, the one to be reversed by a spiritual change, or resurrection to a new life of righteousness here—the other by a glorious change wrought at the resurrection of the body from the grave. But with regard to those of Adam's posterity, who would not, as he did, accept of the gracious terms that should be proposed to them, the original sentence stands in full force, as if it never had been reversed; the word death still includes in it to them the eternal death likewise—everlasting exclusion from the presence of the Lord, and from the glory of his power: for this death, which is the final wages of unexpiated sin, is put in opposition by the Apostle to that "eternal life, which is the gift of God through Jesus Christ our Lord"[3]—so must evidently be eternal as the life to which it is opposed. This penalty then was denounced, has been incurred, and must therefore be inflicted; nor less so, because God is merciful as well as just, for

---

[1] Gen. ii, 17.   [3] Rom. vi, 23.

until his justice is satisfied, we neither are nor can be proper objects of his mercy. Unless then there has been some interposition on our behalf, our case is desperate; and yet, who can interpose? By man came sin—by man therefore must come the satisfaction; and whoever is accepted as our representative, must not only be without sin, work all righteousness in our stead, and sustain the vengeance due to the sins of the whole race of mankind—but must have infinite merit also, to make that righteousness and those sufferings effectual, since without such infinite merit neither can be accepted or imputed, accepted of God the Father, or imputed to us: if Aaron had interposed without his incense, his interposition had been in vain. And who then is sufficient for these things? If any mere man now was as righteous as Adam was created, his righteousness could only save himself, he would not have the least jot or tittle more than the Judge of the world would require of him. But the scriptures have, on the contrary, concluded all men under sin, saying—"All have sinned, and come short of the glory of God;"[1] and again another scripture saith—"None," no mere man, "can by any means redeem his brother, nor give to God a ransom for him;" assigning withal the reason—for the redemption of their soul is precious, of too great price for any man to pay, and it ceaseth for ever,[2] he should never be able to pay it. As yet then we can find no

---

[1] Rom. iii, 23.   [2] Ps. xlix, 7.

satisfaction for sin. For that a righteous man, if any mere man now was so, should have sufficient righteousness to make another righteous—or, that a sinner, as every mere man is, should have any righteousness for another when he has none for himself,—or, that he, who has no righteousness to fulfil the law, should have merit to atone for the transgressions of it,—all this is absurd, contradictory, irreconcileable, and impossible. Whence I infer, that the interposition of Christ alone is sufficient for the accomplishment of this merciful work. And his interposition is indeed every way sufficient. Our Lord Jesus Christ is both God and man,[1] the second person of the eternal Godhead, "of the same substance with the Father," as well as " very man, of the substance of his mother ;" by which union of the divine and human natures in one person, the righteousness he wrought as man was the righteousness of God,[2] and the sufferings he sustained as man were the sufferings of God—for though God cannot suffer, yet he that suffered was God. This is the substance of our faith in this point, and the ground of everlasting consola-

---

[1] Gen. xviii, 1, 13, 14, 17, etc. ; xxxii, 24, 30 ; Exod. xv, 3 ; Josh. v, 13, 14, 15 ; 2 Sam. xxiii, 4 ; Ps. xix, 4, 5 ; xlv, 6, 7 ; Isaiah vii, 14. (Compare Matth. i, 23) ; ix, 6 ; Micah v, 2 ; Zech. xiii, 7 ; Matth. xxii, 44, 45. (Compare Rev. xxii, 16) ; John i, 1, 3, 4, 14 ; iii, 13 ; 1 Epist. iv, 3 ; 1 Tim. iii, 16.

[2] "This is his name whereby he shall be called, Jehovah our Righteousness."—Jer. xxiii, 6.

tion. For here we shall soon find every qualification required. Is the party offended the most righteous God? So is the party who undertakes the mediation, equal in all respects to the Father, as touching his Godhead.[1] Was the offence infinitely sinful, because committed against the most high God? The most high God made the satisfaction,[2] which was therefore infinitely meritorious. Was it committed in human nature? In the same nature was it satisfied—" God was manifest in the flesh, to destroy the works of the devil."[3] As man, he did no sin[4]—" Therefore as by the offence of one (the first Adam) judgement came upon all men to condemnation, even so by the righteousness of one (the second Adam) the free gift came upon all men, unto justification of life; for as by one man's disobedience many were made sinners, so by the obedience of one (imputed to them) shall many be made righteous."[5] "He bare our sins in his own body on the tree."[6] Though he did no sin himself, he took upon him the sins of the whole world; though he was not a sinner by actual transgression in the least degree, yet was he by imputation in the highest:—so that God punished not the innocent for the guilty, as men ignorant of scripture vainly dream; no—the Father found our sins upon him, who of his infinite love had taken them from us, and from the surety now be-

---

[1] John x, 30. [2] 1 John iii, 16. [3] 1 John iii, 8.
[4] 1 Pet. ii, 22. [5] Rom. v, 17, 18, 19.
[6] 1 Pet. ii, 24, from Isaiah liii, 5.

come the debtor, most righteously demanded the debt. This the scriptures everywhere affirm. The scape-goat " bare all the iniquities of the children of Israel;"[1] and upon its great anti-type Jehovah " laid the iniquities of us all."[2] In the vision of Zechariah the high priest Joshua (or Jesus, *i.e.*, the Saviour) the son of Josedech (which is, being interpreted, the son of the essence, the justifier) is represented to the Prophet as clothed with the filthy garments of our sins; and, upon the removal of the filthy garments from him, Jehovah said unto him, "Behold, I have caused thine iniquity to pass from thee,"[3] etc. Whence it is plain, that he was invested with our iniquity, and that the iniquity he was so invested with became his. So likewise in the New Testament it is written—" God made him (to be) sin for us, who knew no sin, that we might be made the righteousness of God in him."[4] He, who knew no sin of his own, became a sinner by investiture with our sins; he was made a sinner in the same sense that we were made righteous; he a sinner by imputation, as we are righteous by imputation; he a sinner by our imputed sins, as we are righteous by his imputed righteousness. We have redemption thereof through his blood, " and by his stripes we are healed."[5] For as he who paid this satisfaction was God as well as man, the satisfaction was on that

---

[1] Levit. xvi, 21, 22.   [2] Isaiah liii, 6.   [3] Zech. iii, 3, 4.
[4] 2 Cor. v, 21.   [5] 1 Pet. ii, 24.

account full and complete, proportionable to the sins of the whole world, and infinite as the justice that required it. Thus, upon the Christian plan, is the most righteous God reconciled to miserable sinners; and the deist, it is to be hoped, will take this matter into serious consideration—upon what other terms the justice and truth of God can admit of the exercise of his mercy. If none shall appear, as I am confident there will not, he will surely be prevailed upon to seek that blessed kingdom of his grace, where "he is JUST, and yet the JUSTIFIER of him which believeth in Jesus;" "where mercy and truth are met together, righteousness and peace have kissed each other."

And now to conclude with an application of the great and leading subject of this discourse. The way to profit by an example is to make the case our own; and whether we make this or not, it will most undoubtedly be so one day, when what is recorded of Israel for our use shall be fulfilled in us as well as them, when all the particulars of this history, how awful soever, shall have a much more awful accomplishment, such as neither I can describe to you, nor you fully conceive. When, instead of the earthly pit opening its mouth to swallow up Korah and his company, the infernal pit of everlasting destruction shall disclose its bottomless depth, to receive alive into it the great adversary, and all that have taken part with him against God, every rebel against Christ and the Christian covenant, from the beginning of time. When, instead of the fire from the presence of the Lord, to consume the two hundred and fifty that offered incense, " Behold the day cometh that shall burn as an oven, and all the proud, yea and all that do wickedly, shall be as stubble, and the day that cometh shall burn them up, saith the Lord of hosts, that it shall leave them neither root nor branch."[1] When, instead of the pestilence to destroy fourteen thousand only of his murmuring people, the inexhaustible floods of Almighty vengeance, heaped up for ages, shall be poured out, to drown in irresistible perdition the innumerable armies of blasphemers, who, in the madness of diabolical pride, and conceited ignorance of fleshly wisdom, dared to charge the All-wise with folly, the Almighty with weakness, disliking his dispensations, and disputing his government. Then (the heavens melting all around, the fiery gulph rolling beneath, and the earth upon which you stand sinking down in flames in the midst)—then will be known the infinite value of Christ's mediation. If any think to shelter themselves in that day behind the strange incense of their own merit, they have seen the event already, they have placed themselves among the dead. But if any such now hear me, let me intreat them to consider well the end of this history, which was recorded in mercy to them, as well as to confirm the hope of the people of God, to

---

[1] Mal. iv, 1.

bring them to the same blessed state the others are possessed of. It is a warning from heaven to flee from the wrath to come. As none but those, whom Aaron protected, escaped the visitation in this history, so none but those whom our great High Priest shall protect, will be able to stand in that day. His all-prevailing merit will be the only plea of the justified, and by his righteousness they will be saved: as he himself declares in that divine book, which was written, as all the visitations in it were sent and recorded, to establish this fundamental doctrine of justification by the righteousness of Christ—to withdraw man, as he says, from his purpose (Hebrew, from working, from working out his own justification), and to hide pride from man (whence the thought of working out his own justification proceeds)—in which divine book, written for this great end, the Redeemer himself expressly declares that, if in the hour of extreme distress, upon which the sinner's acceptance or rejection in the day of final visitation depends, if (then) there be a messenger with him, the great messenger or angel of the covenant,[1] an interpreter, or mediator,[2] one among a thousand, the great captain of our salvation,[3] "to shew unto man His uprightness, then he is gracious to him, and saith, "Deliver him from going down to the pit, for I have found a ransom."[4] And will any refuse to

---

[1] Mal. iii, 1.   [2] 1 Tim. ii, 5.   [3] Josh. v, 14, 15.
[4] Job. xxxiii, 22, 23, 24.

accept of this ransom, and venture their everlasting condition upon an uncertainty? Or do they hope to make their choice then, when "the plague is begun among the people?" When he, who, in the day of grace, long-suffering, and trial, indeed, would not break the humble reed that was bruised, or quench the lighted flax if it did but smoke, shall come, to send forth judgement unto victory, and to be avenged of his enemies? Is this the time for his enemies to submit—for rebels to claim the benefit of an act of grace? The term limited by the act will be expired, the application be too late—"Because I have called," says the judge, "and ye refused, I have stretched out my hand, and no man regarded; but ye have set at nought all my counsel, and would none of my reproof; I also will laugh at your calamity, I will mock when your fear cometh, when your fear cometh as desolation, and your destruction cometh as a whirlwind, when distress and anguish cometh upon you. Then shall they call upon me, but I will not answer, they shall seek me early, but they shall not find me; for that they hated knowledge, and did not choose the fear of the Lord."[1] What remains then but that they come in now, while the act of grace affords a protection? "Behold now is the accepted time, now is the day of salvation."[2] The great High Priest stands ready to receive their prayer, and his golden censer hath

---

[1] Prov. i, 22.   [2] 2 Cor. vi, 2.

much incense[1]—the store of his divine merit is as inexhaustible as their provocations have been innumerable; and whenever any of these children of pride, who once rested upon the merit of their own sinful performances, convinced of the unprofitableness of their best services, and seeing no deliverance in anything they can do for themselves—no not in this world, or that which is to come, but only in God reconciled—shall so humble themselves under a sense of their natural corruption, as to stand afar off, in acknowledgment of their unworthiness, instead of drawing near, as they were wont, to demand what they are no way intitled to—and shall learn to say with the publican in the gospel—" God, be merciful to me a sinner;"[2] or with the upright, yet not so justified, till he became also the penitent Job—" I abhor (myself) and repent in dust and ashes"[3]— they have a gracious assurance in the divine book before cited, which was intended as an antidote to deism to the end of the world, that their petition, preferred in the bitterness of a sincerely-afflicted heart, shall be heard, that they shall be rescued from everlasting death, and their redemption end in glorification; for so it follows in the place above referred to in the book of Job, " He looketh upon men, and if any say, I have sinned, etc., he will deliver his soul from going into the pit, and his life shall see the light."[4]

---

[1] Rev. viii, 3.
[2] Luke xviii, 13.
[3] Job xlii, 6.
[4] Job xxxiii, 27, 28.

To the redeemed of the Lord this history is a sure earnest of their deliverance; and being an additional evidence of their hope, affords fresh matter for their practice. Such as were the sentiments of the surviving Israelites in the dreadful hour of visitation, such now and ever will their's be of their divine benefactor. And what consolation and refreshment of soul, what gratitude and thankfulness must there have been in Israel, which felt the virtue of the atoning censer on the very brink of destruction; a faint, however expressive image of the holy exultation of the Israel of God, when the same divine merits shall be interposed on their behalf at the revelation of God's righteous judgement, the most awful and tremendous scene the eyes of angels or men ever beheld! when he, who delivered them from the corruptions of a sinful world, shall deliver them from the ruins of a burning one; and having, by the all-subduing efficacy of his mighty working, changed misery and death into life and glory,[1] shall place them in a blessed security in the highest heavens, beyond the reach of evil for ever. Let them rejoice then in this glorious hope, hope of deliverance in the day of God, and, in faith thereof, now begin the song they are to take up through the endless day of eternity. Let the Church militant here below learn to sing of the Church triumphant above; and upon all among you, who have this faith and hope in the

---

[1] Phil. iii, 21.

Redeemer of ages, I now solemnly call to join the heavenly chorus of angels and "spirits of just men made perfect," who sung a new song, as he that heard it testifieth, in a language no uninspired tongue ever attained unto, saying (and let us join our grateful voices with their's), saying, "Thou wast slain, and hast redeemed us to God by thy blood, out of every kindred, and tongue, and people, and nation; and hast made us unto our God kings and priests; and we shall reign on the earth. And I beheld, and I heard the voice of many angels round about the throne, and the beasts, and the elders; and the number of them was ten thousand times ten thousand, and thousands of thousands; saying with a loud voice" (and let us never cease to proclaim it, as they do) " Worthy is the Lamb that was slain, to receive power, and riches, and wisdom, and strength, and honour, and glory, and blessing. And every creature which is in heaven, and on the earth, and under the earth, and such as are in the sea, and all that are in them, heard I saying" (and it is therefore our bounden duty to say it) " Blessing, and honour, and glory, and power, (be) unto him that sitteth upon the throne, and unto the Lamb for ever and ever."[1]

Now to God the Father, who justified us,[2] God the Son, who is our righteousness,[3] and God the

---

[1] Rev. v, 9, etc.   [2] Rom. iii, 26.
[3] Jerem. xxiii, 6; 1 Cor. i, 30.

Holy Spirit, who is the sanctifier of all that are justified[1]—the God of infinite love and mercy, who keepeth his promise for ever—the God of peace, order, and union, who maketh men to be of one mind in the house of his Church,[2] the ever blessed and eternal Trinity—be ascribed all the glory of his saints' attainments here, while they are labouring in hope, and of what they shall be, when crowned hereafter in the fulness of joy, for ever and ever. Amen.

---

[1] Rom. xv, 16.
[2] Rom. xv, 5, 6 ; Phil. ii, 2 ; Acts ii, 1, 4, 32.

THE DOCTRINE

OF THE

EVER-BLESSED TRINITY

PROVED IN

A DISCOURSE

ON THE

EIGHTEENTH CHAPTER OF GENESIS.

BY

GEORGE WATSON, M.A.

"Observe here then attentively, attentively observe, that they which appeared unto him (Abraham) were three, and that, after having been said to subsist each with a consistence (meaning a distinct personality) of his own, they are comprehended into one by a word (expressive) of sameness of substance, and for this reason purposely discourse in the manner above-related (i.e., as three and yet as one)."—S. CYRIL. ALEX. CONTR. JULIAN., lib. i, p. 20, vol. vi. Edit. Lutet. 1638.

"Some three months after this, the three Persons in the Trinity dine with Abraham, and foretell the birth of Isaac again."—DR. LIGHTFOOT, vol. i, p. 13.

"The three Persons in the Trinity, in the shape of three men, appear to Abraham, and dine with him."—PAGE 695.

LONDON:

PRINTED FOR E. WITHERS, AT THE SEVEN STARS, BETWEEN THE TEMPLE GATES IN FLEET STREET, AND S. PARKER AND R. CLEMENTS, IN OXFORD.

M.DCC.LVI.

PREFACE.

As the subject of the following sheets has not, I fear, been considered by the generality of readers, it may be advisable, before we proceed, in order to awaken the attention of some, remove the prejudices of others, and satisfy every doubt and scruple of the well-disposed humble mind, to open the way for what is to follow by a few plain passages of holy Scripture, where the divinity of the person or persons in appearances of this kind is expressly ascertained and determined. Let me only first observe, as the person or persons in such appearances are frequently styled ANGELS as well as men, and, particularly, as the Apostle, in the thirteenth chapter to the Hebrews,[1] as well as Moses, calls the three men who appeared to Abraham by this title, that the word for angel in the original Hebrew, and the word angel itself in the Greek, whence we have borrowed it, is well known to be a name of office, and not of nature,[2]

---

[1] Verse 2.

[2] "Dictus est quidem magni consilii angelus, id est, nuntius, *officii*, non *naturæ* vocabulo. Magnum enim cogitatum patris, super hominis scilicet restitutione, annuntiaturus

signifying any agent or messenger, any person or thing delegated, sent, or executing a part in any plan or design; for which reason it is applied in holy Scripture to the heavens, the delegated rulers or agents in the natural world.[1] To the spritual and divine agents in the œconomy of grace. To God the Father,[2] as co-operating with the other divine persons in the stupendous work of our salvation; however, in the order of the œconomy he cannot be sent by them as they are by him; though such sending on his part, and being sent on theirs, in as much as the terms are purely œconomical, *i.e.* relative to the covenant-acts and offices of each, imply no subordination or inferiority of nature, as men ignorant of the Christian covenant blasphemously affirm. To our blessed Lord, who is styled the angel,[3] the messenger, angel, or ambassador (for which the Hebrew word is

---

seculo erat. He (Christ) is called the angel of the great covenant, that is, the messenger, a name of *office*, not of *nature*; because he was to be sent to declare to the world the great plan of the Father, to wit, concerning the restoration of man."—Tertull. de carn. Christ., c. 14.

[1] Psalm ciii, 20, 21; civ, 4; cxlviii, 2; in their primary or literal sense, understood of the *natural* creation.

[2] Gen. xviii, 1, 2; Heb. xiii, 2.

[3] In the following and other places, besides those referred to here and in the sermon—Gen. xxii, 11, 12, 15, 16; xxiv, 7; Exod. xiv, 19, 24, 26; Numb. xxii, 22, 35 (compare verse 38); Judges ii, 1; 1 Chron. xxi, 15, 16, 17; Job xxxiii, 23; Daniel vi, 22; Zechariah iii, i, 3; xii, 8; Luke i, 11, 19, 26; ii, 9; John v, 4; Acts xii, 7; Rev. x, 1.

the same) of the covenant;[1] the angel of the presence,[2] or intercessor; the archangel,[3] or prince of angels. To the Holy Spirit,[4] the sanctifier and comforter, his coadjutor in the covenant of grace,[5] and to the prophets and apostles of our Lord,[6] his evangelists, bishops,[7] etc., the ambassadors[8] in his spiritual kingdom, the gracious subject of whose blessed ministry is emphatically styled εὐαγγέλιον, evangelium, the glad tidings or joyful message—as well as to the good and bad spirits, or agents, commonly understood by the expression.

---

[1] Mal. iii, 1.

[2] Isaiah lxiii, 9 (compare Heb. ix, 24, and Rev. viii, 3); Zech. i, 12.

[3] Jude — 9 (compare Zech. iii, 2, where Jehovah is expressly affirmed to speak the words St. Jude here ascribeth to Michael the archangel—"Jehovah said, Jehovah rebuke thee"—one of the innumerable demonstrations in the book of God of a personality in the divine nature); Dan. x, 21, and Rev. xii, 7, 19; 1 Thess. iv, 16 (compare John v, 28).

[4] Gen. xix, 1, and as I judge with all humility, in Dan. x, 10, 11, 12, 13, 14, 18, 19, 20, 21 (compared with Luke xxii, 43, and Ephes. iii, 16).

[5] Psalm civ, 30, in the spiritual sense; Prov. i, 23; Ezek. xxxvi, 27; Dan. x, 21; John xv, 26; xvi, 14; Acts i, 2; Rom. viii, 9, 10, 11.

[6] Hag. i, 13; Mal. iii, 1; Gal. iv, 4; Rev. xxii, 6 (compare v. 9); Psalm civ, 4, in the SPIRITUAL sense of it, understood of the spiritual creation (compare Heb. i, where the PROPHETS in the first verse are styled ANGELS in the 4th, 7th, and 14).

[7] 2 Tim. iv, 5; Rev. i, 20; ii, 1, 8, 12, 18; iii, 1, 7, 14.

[8] 2 Chron. xxxvi, 15, 16; Mal. ii, 7; 2 Cor. v, 20; Ephes. iv, 11; vi, 20.

No just exception therefore can lie against the application of the word angel, thus explained, to any assumed appearances of the deity, since the divine persons, in these their œconomical acts and gracious manifestations of themselves, are undoubtedly so styled in holy writ; and the context will always determine with the nicest exactness, when the person or persons in such appearances are only created angels or messengers (such, for instance, as the multitude of the heavenly host, which appeared with the angel at our Lord's nativity) or properly divine persons as well as the appearance they assume. That the context doth always decide this, whether the person or persons that appear are styled angels or men (angels from their office, as performing their parts in the great œconomy of redemption, or men, from the form in which they manifested themselves to the bodily eyes of those that beheld them) will be clear, beyond all reasonable controversy, from the following plain passages in holy writ, cited, as was proposed, to prove the divinity of the persons in such appearances. And the

First, I shall mention is Gen. xvi, 13, where Hagar, Sarah's handmaid, affirmeth the angel of the LORD (whom the inspired historian himself likewise in this chapter calleth the angel of the LORD and Jehovah)[1] who found her by the fountain of water in the wilderness, to be GOD. For so we read: "And she

---

[1] Verse 7, 13.

called the name of Jehovah, that spake unto her (*i.e.* him, who was styled the angel of the LORD in the 7th verse) Thou God seest me."[1]

2ndly. Melchizedec, who met Abraham returning from the slaughter of the kings, and blessed him, bringing forth the sacred Christian symbols of bread and wine (Gen. xiv, Heb. vii) was the same divine appearance, exhibited in the united characters of king and high priest. First, being by interpretation king of righteousness, and after that also king of Salem, which is not meant here of any city so called, being purposely interpreted to shew it is not so meant, but is king of peace; which, with the other high titles and essential properties that follow, are absolutely incommunicable—without father, without mother, though a man in appearance, yet not of the generation of men—without descent or genealogy, of no stock or family on the earth,—having neither beginning of days nor end of life, being very Jehovah himself, co-eternal with the Father, but made like unto the Son of God, the form, lineaments, etc. he assumed being made exactly to resemble the body prepared him[2] in the days of his flesh, even that holy thing, which was afterwards begotten of the Holy Ghost, and born of the Virgin Mary.[3] This Melchizedec, of whom such things are spoken, described under characters applicable to no mere man that ever came into the world; after whose order (Gr. κατα

---

[1] Gen. xvi, 13.   [2] Heb. x, 5.   [3] Luke i, 35.

ταξιν, according to whose institution, and exact similitude,[1] as he was before his incarnation exhibited to Adam, Noah, Abraham, etc.) our great high-priest accordingly arose in the flesh in the fulness of time; unto whom so exhibited even the patriarch Abraham himself, who had the promises, and who was therefore the greatest man upon earth, gave the tenth[2] of the spoils, thereby attributing to him all the glory of his victory; who blessed Abraham, blessed him that had the promises, and without all contradiction the lesser is blessed of the better; to whom Levi paid tithes in the loins of his father Abraham; of whom, in contradistinction to the mortality of the legal priests, it is witnessed (and a testimony of essential divinity it is) that "HE LIVETH." "This Melchizedec, saith the apostle, ABIDETH A PRIEST CONTINUALLY." For take away the apposition, or parenthesis, from the words "king of Salem," in the first verse, to "Son of God," in the second, the grammar of the sentence apparently is—"this Melchizedec abideth a priest continually;" *i.e.*, because he continueth ever, hath an unchangeable priesthood (Gr. απαραβατον ιερωσυνην—a priesthood that passeth not from one to another); and how there could ever be two priests of this kind, how an everlasting high-priest could have a successor, is a contradiction no gloss or commentary upon earth will ever be able to

---

[1] Heb. vii, 15.
[2] See Gen. xxviii, 22, where the patriarch *Jacob* voweth the same unto *God*.

reconcile. And therefore I conclude, this appearance to Abraham, and the after-appearance of the Son of God, in the flesh, to the children of Abraham, was the one true priest of the most high God, the one Mediator between God and man, JESUS CHRIST, the same yesterday, to-day, and for ever.[1]

To which this will be a proper place to add,

3rdly. That Elihu, whose sudden appearance is introduced to determine the case Job and his three disputing friends were not able to bring to an issue, and thereby the great end and design of that holy book against the deist and disputer of this world in all ages, though manifested in the shape and character of a young man, could be no other than the Son of God; being first Elihu, which is, by interpretation, my God himself, and then, the only-begotten of the Father, Son of Barachel, which is Son of the blessed God; in whose awful presence Job and his three friends, so ready to answer before, opened not their mouths,—they were amazed, they answered no more, they left off speaking;[2] who expressly styleth the Holy Ghost by the œconomical title of his father—saying, "The spirit of God hath made me, and the breath of the Almighty hath given me life;"[3] plainly assuming to himself in the next verse but one, the mediatorial office and character: "Behold, I (am) according to thy wish, in God's

---

[1] Heb. xiii, 8. [2] Job xxxii, 15.
[3] Job xxxiii, 4.

stead, I also am formed out of the clay. Behold, my terror shall not make thee afraid, neither shall my hand be heavy upon thee,"[1]—the power of re-instating man in original righteousness—" Speak, for I desire to justify thee,"[2]—and the attribute of infinite wisdom—" He that is perfect in knowledge (is) with thee ;"[3] who evidently taketh up and pursueth at the beginning of the thirty-eighth chapter, in the character of Jehovah out of the whirlwind, the great and glorious argument for the abasement of human pride, *viz.*, the consideration of God's stupendous wisdom and power displayed in the visible creation, which he had entered upon, for the same purpose, towards the end of the thirty-sixth chapter in the character of Elihu ; and of whom Job himself finally testifieth, that he was the person whose frequent appearances had been handed down by tradition, as the inspired writer of the history doth, that the words supposed to contain this testimony were addressed to Jehovah himself—for so we read in the forty-second chapter, in the account of Job's penitential confession, —" Then Job answered Jehovah, and said," etc., " I have heard of thee by the hearing of the ear, but now mine eye seeth thee ;"[4] which words, taken together, being an express declaration that Job then saw Jehovah, and Jehovah himself dwelling in the light which no man can approach unto, " whom no man hath seen or can see,"[5] must be understood of

---

[1] Job. xxxiii, 6. [2] Job ver. 32. [3] *Ibid.* xxxvi, 4.
[4] *Ibid.* ver. 1, 6. [5] 1 Tim. vi, 16.

some visible exhibition of Jehovah, as he was used to manifest himself in those days—and of whom, of all the parties present, can we possibly understand this, but of Elihu? In which case we have this farther evidence, if more be necessary, of his divinity, that Job's penitential confession is made to him, with the additional acknowledgement of his divine attributes—" I know that thou canst do every(thing) and (that) no thought can be witholden from thee."¹

4thly. The angels of God, which met Jacob on his way from Padan-aram, as you find it recorded in the thirty-second chapter of Genesis, whatever glorious retinue might, as at Sinai,² accompany them, were undoubtedly, I think, a divine appearance. For, first, the patriarch gives the place a name in memory of this heavenly vision, an honour he would hardly have paid to mere created angels, but which it was the patriarchal custom, in gratitude for mercies received, and for prophetic purposes, to pay to God himself, as, to mention no more, the patriarch Jacob did at Beth-el and Peni-el.³ Secondly, consider the name itself he gave the place, viz., Mahanaim, i.e., 'hosts' or 'camps,' " Because," said he, " this is God's host," or encampment;⁴ and we read in the thirty-fourth Psalm, "The angel of the LORD encampeth round about them that fear him," (or, that I may not seem to take advantage of the translation, as the

---

¹ Tim. xlii, 2. ² Ps. lxviii, 17.
³ Gen. xxviii, 19 ; and xxxii, 30. ⁴ Verse 2.

word is different in the Hebrew, causeth them to be *surrounded,* or *encompassed,* that fear him, by way of protection, which comes to the same) " and delivereth them."[1] Thirdly, the prophet Elisha, who was himself visibly surrounded with one of those heavenly encampments, as we read, 2 Kings vi, 17, has, in his exhortation to his desponding servant, given us the spiritual design or intention of them, thereby leaving us the best comment upon what Jacob intended by Mahanaim, *viz.,* that such visible exhibitions of divine protection, agreeable to the miraculous dispensation of those times, were figures of the invisible support then and at all times vouchsafed to the servants of God.—" He answered, fear not ; for they that (be) with us," meaning the horses and chariots of fire round about him, which his servants' eyes were opened to behold, " are more than they that (be) with them."[2] The full sense of which is expressed by St. John in that sweet and comfortable assurance—" Ye are of GOD, little children, and have overcome them, because greater is he that is in you, than he that is in the world."[3] From all which, laid together, and duly weighed, as this divine support is the office of the Holy Comforter in the œconomy of grace, we may reasonably infer the manifestation of two of the divine persons on this occasion to the patriarch Jacob ; who, with their attending hosts, visibly encamped round about him, in type and

---

[1] Gen. xxviii, 7.   [2] Verse 16.   [3] 1 St. John iv, 4.

figure then, as they still invisibly encamp about and protect every believer on his way to Heaven.

5thly. Again; the man who wrestled with the patriarch Jacob, as you find it recorded in the same chapter, is expressly styled God by himself and the patriarch, and by the prophet Hosea both God and the Angel. He telleth the patriarch, who had power with him, that he had power with God.[1] The patriarch saith to him, "I will not let thee go, except thou bless me;" and we read, "he blessed him there,"[2] which no one but God could do in his own name. The patriarch calleth the name of the place Peni-el. "For," saith he, "I have seen God face to face."[3] And the prophet Hosea, speaking of the patriarch Jacob concerning this wonderful transaction, expressly declareth of him—"By his strength he had power with God, yea he had power over the angel, and prevailed; he wept and made supplication unto him, he found him in Beth-el, and there he spake with us, even Jehovah, God of hosts, Jehovah is his memorial."[4]

6thly. The same holy patriarch, in his blessing of the two sons of Joseph, related Gen. xlviii, 15, calleth the God of his fathers the Angel which redeemed him, saying, as it is there written :—"And he blessed Joseph and said, God, before whom my fathers Abraham and Isaac did walk, the God, which fed me

---

[1] Gen. xxxii, 28.   [2] Verse 26, 29.   [3] Verse 30.
[4] Hos. xii, 3.

all my life long unto this day—the angel which redeemed me from all evil—bless the lads."[1]

7thly. The angel who appeared unto Moses in a flame of fire out of the midst of the bush, Exod. iii, 2, Acts vii, 30-5, is over and over again declared to be JEHOVAH and GOD. " For the angel of the Lord appeared to him,"[2] " and when Jehovah saw that he turned aside to see, God called unto him ;"[3] " moreover he said I (am) the God of thy fathers, the God of Abraham, the God of Isaac, and the God of Jacob —and Moses hid his face, for he was afraid to look upon God.[4] The angel of the LORD therefore in this appearance was Jehovah and God ; and so, let me add here, was the Man that appeared to Joshua, when he was by Jericho,[5] the captain, or prince, of the host of Jehovah, as he is styled in this scripture,[6] or, as by the prophet Daniel, "Michael their prince."[7] For Joshua fell on his face to the earth and did worship ; and he addressed Joshua in the very same words that the angel of the Lord spake to Moses from the bush, " Loose thy shoe from off thy foot, for the place whereon thou standest is holy—and Joshua did so."[8]

8thly. That the appearance on the mount, at the giving of the law, was divine, cannot be questioned. For Mount Sinai was altogether on a smoke, because

---

[1] Hosea xii, 15, 16. [2] Exod. iii, 2. [3] Verse 4.
[4] Verse 6. [5] Josh. v, 13. [6] Josh. v, 15.
[7] Dan. x, 21 ; xii, 1. [8] Verse 15 (compare Exodus iii, 5).

Jehovah descended upon it in fire, in all the terror of the divine majesty, such as he is and ever will be to every unjustified transgressor of the law, in the known outward emblem or figure of divine wrath, which is in itself inconceivable, "and the smoke thereof ascended as the smoke of a furnace, and the whole mount quaked greatly. And when the voice of the trumpet sounded long, and waxed louder and louder" (which shall again be heard " with the voice of the archangel,"[1] when he cometh in like manner to judge the transgressors of his law) " Moses spake, and God answered him by a voice."[2] " Whose voice then shook the earth ; but now he hath promised, saying, yet once more I shake not the earth only, but also heaven."[3] " From whose face, at his next coming, the earth and the heaven shall flee away, and there shall be found no place for them."[4] And yet this awful and tremendous appearance, whose voice, speaking out of the midst of the fire, Israel could not endure,[5] before whom Moses himself, though appointed a representative of Christ,—a typical mediator and intercessor between Jehovah and his Church,[6] "so terrible was the sight, that Moses said, I exceedingly fear and quake,"[7]—this Almighty Creator and Judge of the world, I say, who is styled JEHOVAH and GOD in this scripture, and in Psalm lxviii,

---

[1] Thess. iv, 16.   [2] Exod. xix, 18, 19.   [3] Heb. xii, 26.
[4] Revelations xx, 11.   [5] Deuteronomy v, 25.
[6] Deut. v, 5 ; Gal. iii, 19.   [7] Heb. xii, 21.

God, IAH (he that IS) and the God of Israel, is by his holy martyr St. Stephen, under immediate inspiration, called by his œconomical title of the Angel, where, speaking of Moses, he expressly saith—" This is he that was in the church in the wilderness, with the angel that spake to him in the mount Sina," etc., " who received the lively oracles, to give unto us."[1]

9thly. That the angel, who appeared to Gideon, mentioned in the sixth chapter of the book of Judges, and the angel, who appeared in like manner to Manoah, the father of Sampson, mentioned in the thirteenth chapter, was not only the same, but the same also with the above-described appearances, will be evident from a comparison of the two chapters, and the many undoubted proofs given of his divinity in both. It will be sufficient for my purpose however, after what is said already, just to take notice, that he is styled in both places, as above, the angel of the Lord, and the angel of God; that, upon his appearance to Gideon, he saith, " Jehovah (is) with thee, thou mighty man of valour;"[2] and upon Gideon's affectionate remonstrance, as if Jehovah had forsaken his people and delivered them into the hands of their enemies, it is said, Jehovah " looked upon him, and said, Go in this thy might, and thou shalt save Israel from the hand of the Midianites, have I not sent thee? Surely, I will be with thee;"[3] that he answereth Manoah's enquiry about his name by

---

[1] Acts vii, 38. [2] Judg. vi, 12. [3] Ver. 14, 16.

declaring it to be "secret," or "wonderful,"[1] one of the express titles of Christ in the prophet Isaiah;[2] in a word, that both Gideon and Manoah sacrifice to him, Gideon a kid and unleavened cakes, Manoah a kid with a meat-offering, and that he accepteth of their sacrifices, expressly commanding the latter, who did not know him at first to be the angel of the Lord, to offer his sacrifice to him as Jehovah;[3] and lastly, that, upon his being known to both to be the angel of the Lord by his miraculous acceptance of their offerings, Gideon said, "Alas, O Lord God, for because I have seen the angel of the Lord face to face—"[4] "And Jehovah said unto him, Peace (be) unto thee, fear not, thou shalt not die;"[5] "and Manoah said unto his wife," which explaineth what Gideon said, "We shall surely die, because we have seen God."[6]

The reader will be pleased to observe, that in all the above passages of holy writ, either the divine names, Jehovah or God, or some divine title or attribute, are mentioned; some miracle of divine power wrought; or some promise, requiring the exertion of such divine power for the accomplishment thereof, given; some act of religious adoration accepted; a sameness of form, lineaments, etc., in the appearance; or, in a word, some well-known token, some manifestation of the divine presence displayed,

---

[1] Judg. xiii, 18.   [2] Isa. ix, 6.   [3] Judg. xiii, 16.
[4] See Gen. xxxii, 30.   [5] Judg. vi, 22, 23.   [6] xiii, 22.

whereby the persons, honoured with such appearances, might distinguish them from all other appearances whatever; as is evident, not only in the case of the holy patriarchs, prophets, high-priest, etc., but even in those of Abimelech[1] and Nebuchadnezzar, who were heathen princes, the latter of whom expressly declareth, of himself, without any particular information at the time—"And the form of the fourth is like the Son of God;"[2] whom the king, very remarkably for our purpose, at the 28th verse, calleth the Angel of God—" (Then) Nebuchadnezzar spake and said, Blessed (be) the God of Shadrach," etc., "who hath sent his angel, and delivered his servants that trusted in him."

If it should be doubted, whether the instances above given are conclusive in the present case, in as much as the appearances therein recorded are all to be referred to the second person, whom the primitive fathers generally suppose to have appeared on such occasions, I shall beg leave to remark, in hopes of throwing some additional light on what those holy men have left us upon this subject, that, though it was generally the second person only that appeared, it was not always; as is, I think, sufficiently evident from the two instances produced in the following discourse. Generally speaking indeed it was, and for these obvious reasons, because he was to be one day incarnate, and by his incarnation become, as the

---

[1] Gen. xx, 3, 4. [2] Dan. iii, 25.

prophet testifieth of him, the angel, or messenger of the covenant; but then the reader will always bear in mind, as it is of the utmost consequence he should, that whenever Jehovah or God (אלהים, plural) is said to appear, the undivided power and glory of the co-eternal Trinity was always present, however, in their infinite wisdom, one or more of the persons might be manifested under a visible form, as the œconomical appropriation of offices or design of each particular manifestation required.

Innumerable instances more might be added from the scriptures both of the Old and New Testament; but the few I have already set down, with the above hints for laying the several proofs in scripture together, will be a clue to direct any further enquiries the reader may choose to make for himself. Of what I have written, as well as of the following discourse, I have only to say, that I thought it might be of some little service to the public at this time; and hope it will be received as my humble mite thrown into the treasury of God (to be succeeded by others as I shall see occasion and God shall give me ability) towards the support of those orthodox Creeds, and that most admirable Liturgy which, upheld against the secret underminings of the present age by the same Almighty Hand that rescued them from the open violence of the last, have preserved this beautiful garden of the Church of England from being turned into a common; and by which, together with her truly apostolical form of government by bishops (no honours or privileges conferred upon the episcopacy by the secular power, how unhappy a temptation soever they may have been to worldly-minded men to usurp a civil authority that doth not belong to the church, or betray the spiritual one that doth, in the least taking away aught from the divine institution and office itself, which descends by consecration, a circumstance some men, it is to be hoped, have not duly considered) by which orthodox Creeds I say, most admirable Liturgy, and truly apostolical form of Government, whatever improvement she might derive from a due exertion of ancient, however now neglected, rights and discipline, and from a restoration of primitive simplicity, increase of faith, and heavenly-mindedness, she is notwithstanding undoubtedly the purest church this day upon earth; in her articles and institutions, the glory of all the churches, daily condemning her unworthy sons from the words of their own mouths, and with the united melody of many faithful hearts yet remaining within her, giving glory to God her Saviour, the King of Glory and of saints, in these last levelling times of anti-christian confusion.

THE DOCTRINE

OF THE

EVER-BLESSED TRINITY.

A SERMON.

GENESIS XVIII, 1, 2.

And the Lord appeared unto him in the plains (Heb., among the oaks) *of Mamre, as he sat in the tent door, in the heat of the day. And he lift up his eyes, and looked, and lo three men stood by him.*

THE learned and pious compilers of our most excellent liturgy having appointed this chapter of Genesis one of the proper lessons for Trinity Sunday, this alone, I should think, would be sufficient to excite our curiosity, and lead us to a diligent enquiry into the reasons for which they appointed it; especially as it is our duty at all times to search the holy scriptures in general for evidence of this great and fundamental doctrine, upon which all our hope of salvation and future glory dependeth. And if ever there was a time, when the absolute necessity of a firm belief of this doctrine should, with more than ordinary zeal and industry, be pressed home to the hearts of the people, it is the age wherein we live;

when not only every little forward vainly-philosophising declaimer, without the least knowledge of his bible, thinks himself qualified to dispute the faith, upon which the church has stood from the beginning, and to blaspheme the adorable name in which he was baptized, (which, whatever he may think of it, is to renounce the faith) but when even a guardian and overseer[1] of the flock of Christ himself, whose high office it is to ordain others to preach the gospel of salvation, *i.e.*, the long and earnestly-expected incarnation of the second person in the ever-blessed Trinity—the revelation of the great and

---

[1] The miserably-deluded, still persisting, and, to the great scandal of the Christian Church and hierarchy, yet unexcommunicated author of the *Essay on Spirit*;* to which I cannot pass by this opportunity of recommending a most complete and admirable answer by my truly-learned friend, and beloved fellow-labourer in the gospel, Mr. William Jones, late of University College in Oxford, printed for E. Withers at the Seven Stars, next the Inner Temple Gate in Fleet Street; and S. Parker, at Oxford, 1753; which not only calleth for the commendation and thanks of every orthodox believer, but whose worthy author (if a private person may with due deference give his judgment in this respect) deserveth some honourable testimony of approbation from the governors of that Church, of the fundamental article whereof, besides the other valuable learning contained in it, it is so seasonable and judicious a defence.

---

* This essay is *ascribed* to Robert Clayton (bishop of Clogher); for further particulars see Darling's *Cyclopædia Bibliographica*, *tit.* Clayton, columns 694-5, and Jones (of Nayland), col. 1683.
—Editor.

glorious mystery of God manifest in the flesh—when one, so stationed by divine consecration for this and the government of God's church, dareth openly to deny the whole of that gospel he sendeth out his clergy to proclaim ; and so, of course, the justification of sinners through the all-prevailing merits of God the Son, and the sanctification of man's fallen nature by the power of God the Holy Ghost—as every one evidently does, and must do, who denieth the divinity of either. It shall be my endeavour therefore in the following discourse, as it ought to be at all times, and eminently at such a time, of every Christian pastor, to guard you against the dangerous influence of such abominable heresy ; and with this view, I will now attempt to shew you, in the plainest manner I am able, the doctrine of a Trinity in Unity, three co-eternal persons and one undivided essence, are clearly revealed to us in this chapter of Genesis. That God often appeared to holy men under the patriarchal and Jewish dispensations, and that he appeared at such times as a man, or men, to remind them of his promised manifestation in the flesh in the fulness of time, must be evident to all who read and believe the sacred history, wherein many of these appearances are circumstantially recorded. That the person, or persons, so appearing were truly and essentially God, may in the several places where they occur be abundantly demonstrated. We will now proceed to consider the arguments for this in the chapter before us ; and the

I. First point I shall endeavour to prove by them is, that the vision here vouchsafed to Abraham was of God Himself. And

1. This is expressly asserted in the beginning of the chapter, in the words of the text. They inform us, as you have heard, that the Lord appeared unto him. The word here translated *Lord* is in the original, *Jehovah;* which, as it signifieth "He that is, that he hath life and all possible perfection in himself, and deriveth them not from another," is a name that cannot without blasphemy be communicated to a creature, the high and distinguishing name of the " Lord God Almighty, which was, and is, and is to come."[1] This being the allowed interpretation of the name Jehovah, and this interpretation manifestly determining it to be the incommunicable property of God, it is as plain as words can make it, that God appeared unto Abraham, for the text saith, " Jehovah appeared unto him."

2. Again; another proof of his divinity who appeared may be drawn from the holy patriarch's behaviour upon the occasion, who immediately, without hesitation, payeth divine honours to him. For so we read in the 6th and 7th verses, which are a plain description of a sacrifice.—"And Abraham hastened into the tent unto Sarah, and said, make ready quickly three measures of fine meal, knead (it) and make cakes upon the hearth. And Abraham ran

---

[1] Rev. iv, 8.

unto the herd, and fetched a calf tender and good, and gave (it) unto a young man, and he hasted to dress it." The Hebrew says "to *sacrifice* it," as the word here translated "to dress it" signifieth, and is rendered by all the translators in abundance of places.[1] Now sacrifice was the highest act of religious worship, instituted as a memorial of that one all-sufficient sacrifice, which was to be offered up in the fulness of time for the sins of the world; and would Abraham, do ye think, sacrifice to any mere men or angels? Would the father of the faithful, in whose seed (*i.e.*, Christ) all the nations of the earth were to be blessed, whose faith shineth so conspicuous throughout the whole history of his life, pay adoration to a false object? This is too great an absurdity to be credited; and yet, great as it is, it will unavoidably follow, unless we suppose this appearance to be Him, to whom alone worship is

---

[1] לעשׂה אתך. עשׂה, pro sacrificare, offerre, etc., to sacrifice, to offer, etc. Marius. See Exod. xxix, 36, 39, 41. So the heathens use the word in Greek and Latin. The reason of this sense of the word so prevailing in all languages was undoubtedly traditional; and if the opinion that this feast was sacrificial, *i. e.*, a meat-offering, needeth any further confirmation, it will receive a great one from a very striking circumstance that is added in the next chapter, to a feast of the same kind made by Lot for two of these three men, or angels.—"And he made them a feast, and baked unleavened bread," etc. See this circumstance in the law concerning the meat-offering, Levit. vi, 16, and for the reason or intention of it, 1 Cor. v, 8.

due. But it may be said—Abraham was mistaken, as St. John undoubtedly was, when he went to worship the angel, as he telleth us in his revelation he did; as the Apostle mistook the glorious messenger he saw for his blessed master, so might the patriarch the three men that appeared to him for divine persons, when they really were not so. The argument then will come to this—either Abraham was mistaken, or the persons he saw were divine; for he certainly supposed them to be so, or he would never have sacrificed to them. But the text, you will recollect, affirmeth that the Lord, or Jehovah, appeared to him. If therefore he believed what the text positively affirmeth (as his actions declare he did), then he was not mistaken when he supposed this appearance to be Jehovah, then it is evident this appearance was Jehovah; which was the thing to be proved.

3. Again; another argument to prove that it was God himself who appeared to Abraham, is, that he who appeareth hath divine attributes ascribed to him; and first, that he is all-knowing—the very thoughts of the heart, and most secret actions of the mind, are here represented as laying open to his sight. For upon his promise of a son to the patriarch, when he and Sarah his wife were old, and she past child-bearing, it is written, that "Sarah heard it in the tent door, which was behind him, and that she laughed within herself;" to which is subjoined: "And Jehovah said unto Abraham, wherefore did

Sarah laugh? Then Sarah denied, saying, I laughed not (for she was afraid). And he (that is, Jehovah) said, Nay but thou didst laugh."[1] What complicated evidence is here of the point under consideration? He that saith this is styled Jehovah; and Sarah laughed within herself. This laughter of Sarah's first appeareth to have been mixed with some degree of human doubt through astonishment; but afterwards we find her heart, upon reflection, filled with the same holy joy Abraham's had been before[2] at so high and, through her means, unexpected a blessing to herself and all the world—insomuch that this great representative of the Christian Church most thankfully and devoutly declareth in faith, upon the accomplishment of the promise, "God hath made me to laugh, so that all that hear will laugh with me."[3] For which reason also the promised seed that was born of her was called Isaac, which word signifieth laughter, as a lively pledge of the promised seed, that was to be born in the fulness of time; at whose birth the angel emphatically said—"Behold I bring you good tidings of great joy, which shall be to all people"[4]—When all that heard and believed did indeed partake of Sarah's joy, and, as she here foretold, "laughed with her." But to proceed with the argument before us—"Sarah laughed within herself"—Now if she had even smiled outwardly,

---

[1] Gen. xviii, 10, 12, 13, 15.   [2] Chap. xvii, 17.
[3] Chap. xxi, 6.   [4] Luke ii, 10.

he that spake could not have seen her, unless he was God, for the Scripture saith, "she was behind him." But this was not the case; for she laughed within herself. Yet though she was behind him, and laughed within herself, he saw her; though she denied it, he convicted her; and who could do this without discerning the thoughts of the heart? And who discerneth the thoughts of the heart but God alone?[1] When our Lord at once knew Nathanael, without being informed who he was, described to him the inward frame and disposition of his soul, and told him he had seen him when Nathanael was certain no man was present, Nathanael immediately acknowledged him to be the Messiah, *i.e.*, God as well as man, from the demonstration he had given of his divinity.[2] Let us imitate the faith of this Israelite indeed, and believe God to be in these three men who appeared unto Abraham; for divine omnipresence and knowledge are as conspicuous in the words here spoken to Sarah, as in those which the Saviour of the world there spoke to Nathanael. But omniscience is not the only attribute here ascribed to the divine speaker; he himself in direct terms likewise asserteth

4. His Omnipotence. "And Jehovah said unto Abraham, Wherefore did Sarah laugh, saying, shall I, of a surety, bear a son which am old? Is anything too hard for Jehovah? At the time appointed

---

[1] 1 Kings viii, 39.   [2] John i, 47-9.

will I return unto thee, according to the time of life and Sarah shall have a son."[1] Doth he not here call himself Jehovah? Doth he not declare all things are possible to him? Doth he not assure Abraham that he would do the miracle, which we know came to pass? Give a due attention to the words, and you will want no further comment upon them—"Is anything too hard for Jehovah? At the time appointed will I return unto thee, and Sarah shall have a son." It will add weight however to the argument just to mention in this place, that when the promise was accomplished, as we read in the twenty-first chapter it was, it is there recorded in these remarkable words—"Jehovah visited Sarah, as He had said, and Jehovah did unto Sarah, as He had spoken."[2] Now compare these two texts together, and see what will be the inference.—"And Jehovah said, Is anything too hard for Jehovah? At the time appointed will I return unto thee, and Sarah shall have a son."—"And Jehovah visited Sarah, as he had said, and Jehovah did unto Sarah, as he had spoken." The plain inference from which is, that if Jehovah visited Sarah, as he had said, then he who said he would return was Jehovah; and if he said, likewise, nothing was too hard for him to effect, then did he in plain terms affirm himself to be Almighty. I will only observe farther, that the time appointed, at which Jehovah saith in the

---

[1] Gen. xviii, 13, 14.   [2] Verse 1.

eighteenth chapter, "I will return unto thee," is in the twenty-first chapter called "the set time of which God had spoken to him."[1]

I have now, I hope, sufficiently proved that the persons who appeared to Abraham were divine—they have the divine incommunicable name, divine honours, and divine attributes; they are Jehovah—they are worshipped by him who is styled the friend of God[2]—they are all-knowing—they are almighty. Their divinity therefore being unquestionable, we must now proceed to shew their personality, that as we have seen there was one Jehovah in this appearance, we may also as clearly discern that they were

II. Three divine persons. Now the

1. First argument I shall bring to prove this will be the words of the text, which are indeed as determinate and conclusive as possible. "Jehovah," it is said, "appeared unto Abraham, and lo! three men stood by him." Were not these three men the "appearance"? And were they not then Jehovah? But to be a little more particular; how did Jehovah appear? for the Scripture saith, "no man hath seen God at any time."[3] Why, it is said, "Abraham lift up his eyes and looked, and lo! three men stood by him." These three men then were Jehovah; the appearance was human, but Jehovah was in the appearance; and the persons in the appearance were

---

[1] Gen. xxi, 2.   [2] James ii, 23.   [3] John i, 18.

three, because the persons in Jehovah are three. A Trinity in Unity therefore is here set forth in the plainest manner to all capacities; and the words speak the same intelligible language, as those of the beloved disciple: "There are THREE which bear record in heaven, the Father, the Word, and the Holy Ghost, and these THREE are one."[1] But

2. Abraham knew this, understood the great mystery (or spiritual truth) represented by this appearance, as is evident from the form of his address. For he "lift up his eyes, and looked, and lo! three men stood by him; and when he saw (them) he ran to meet them from the tent door, and bowed himself toward the ground, and said, My LORD, if now I have found favour in thy sight, pass not away, I pray thee, from thy servant."[2] Here, you see, though there were three men, he addresseth them in the singular number; though he beheld three men standing before him, he calleth the three "my Lord;" he saith not, my Lords, in the plural number, but my Lord, in the singular; he plainly therefore knew the undivided essence of Jehovah to be in the three men who stood before him (for, besides the absurdity of creature-worship, he never would have addressed the three men, as men, with this singular appellation), that though it was in each of them, it was nevertheless undivided; that with respect to their divine nature they were one and the same. But as he

---

[1] 1 John v, 7.   [2] Genesis xviii, 2, 3.

knew the persons that were in the three men to be one Jehovah, so did he of course acknowledge in Jehovah three co-essential persons; for unless he had believed a divine person to have been in each, he would not have worshipped the three men as he did: the divine and eternal, not created and assumed nature, he undoubtedly worshipped, and by paying such divine honour to the three (the three divine persons *in* the three men, as above described) evidently acknowledged in the divine nature three co-eternal co-equal persons. He said my Lord indeed, in the singular number, but he said it to THEM, and the remaining part of his invocation is as remarkably in the plural, of which I shall have occasion to speak more particularly below. To show the personality then in Jehovah—that he was three and yet one, three and one in different respects—three persons and one essence, and at the same time to show the divine persons in their covenant-offices, that each sustained a part in the œconomy of redemption, was manifestly the design of God's condescension in this appearance; this the reason of his appearing in the manner he did upon this occasion, in three men, not in one, as the second person always did, when his incarnation was the only thing to be exhibited. Thus having proved before from Abraham's actions, that he knew the men he saw to be God, I have now proved from his own words, that he knew there was a Trinity of persons in the Godhead; for which I shall subjoin one more authority, amongst many, taken notice of by Zanchius, in his book "Concerning the three Elohim, the eternal Father, Son, and Holy Ghost, one and the same Jehovah." "I pass over," saith he, "what I also have touched upon in the twentieth chapter, where Abraham, speaking to king Abimelech of HIM who had called him out of his own land, saith, And when the Elohim (THEY) caused me to wander from my father's house, etc., for he joineth Elohim with a verb plural, התעו, THEY caused me to wander; and when Moses calleth Jehovah, Abraham calleth Elohim. Did not Abraham therefore KNOW, that JEHOVAH was a PLURALITY of ELOHIM?"[1]

3. The third and last argument I shall propose, is the frequent and promiscuous use of the singular and plural numbers, in the inspired writer's account of these three men and the patriarch. I will briefly collect the passages together, and they will be a striking evidence to you. "Jehovah appeared unto Abraham, and lo! three men stood by him, and when he saw (them) he ran to meet them."[2] The

---

[1] "Taceo hic, quod supra etiam attigi ex cap. 20, ubi Abraham de EO, qui se de suâ terrâ evocaverat, loquens ad regem Abimelechum, ait, quumque errare fecerunt me Elohim a domo patris mei, etc. Nam Elohim cum verbo plurali, התעו, errare fecerunt, conjungit. Et quem Moses vocaverat Jehovam, Abraham vocat Elohim. An non igitur Abrahamus novit, Jehovam Plures esse Elohim?" Hieron. Zanchii de tribus Elohim, æterno Patre, Filio, et Spiritu Sancto, uno eodem que Jehovâ. Lib. ii, cap. 2.

[2] Genesis xviii, 1, 2.

inspired historian here speaketh both in the singular and plural number. "Jehovah," saith he, "appeared unto Abraham, and lo! three men stood by him, etc., and he ran to meet them." Then followeth Abraham's address to them, the first part of which is in the singular number—"And said (he said unto them), My Lord, if I have now found favour in thy sight, pass not away, I pray thee, from thy servant."[1] Here he speaketh all along in the singular number, *i.e.*, he addresseth them as one; but on a sudden, in his invocation of them to partake of the sacrifice, he changeth the number in the very same speech, as followeth—"Let a little water, I pray you, be fetched, and wash your feet (the word your is plural, not singular), and rest yourselves under the tree. And I will fetch a morsel of bread, and comfort ye your hearts; after that ye shall pass on, for therefore are ye come to your servant."[2] All this plainly in the plural number, as the former part of the address was in the singular. 2. The inspired historian likewise expresseth himself in the plural number, and as suddenly changeth it into the singular—"And they said, so do as thou hast said. And Abraham, etc., took butter and milk, and the calf which he had dressed, and set (it) before them, and they did eat. And they said unto him, Where is Sarah thy wife?"[3] All this is in the plural number; what followeth is in the singular. "And he

---

[1] Gen. xviii. 3.   [2] Ver. 4, 5.   [3] Ver. 5, 8, 9.

said, I will certainly return unto thee—And Jehovah said, wherefore did Sarah laugh ? At the time appointed will I return unto thee, etc. Then Sarah denied, saying, I laughed not; and he said, nay but thou didst laugh."[1] This variation in the numbers can, I think, be no way accounted for or reconciled, without supposing the three who appeared to be one in some other respect—three persons and one Jehovah; and I hope enough has been said to prove they were so.

The use the Apostle hath made of this Scripture, to enforce the great duty of Christian hospitality— "Be not forgetful to entertain strangers, for thereby some have entertained angels unawares"[2]—will, to such as consider the allowed signification of the word angel, as above given, that it is, as Tertullian justly observeth, a name of office, not of nature, be no reasonable objection to the above account of this appearance. Rather, on the contrary, the Apostle's argument will derive a peculiar force and emphasis from supposing the angels he referreth to in this passage to be the divine persons themselves—graciously condescending thus to visit the holy fathers of our faith, to foreshew, in figure, that they would one day visit and redeem their people—deigning to be visibly present at the sacred rites they themselves had appointed, as well as to declare they appointed them, as to signify their acceptance of

---

[1] Gen. xviii, 10, 13-15. [2] Heb. xiii, 2.

the one great sacrifice, of whose oblation in the latter days of the world they ordained these as memorials — humbling themselves even to come down from heaven and converse with men, in evidence of the communication between heaven and earth being opened again by the then prevailing virtue of his after-sufferings, who was to cloud the insupportable terror of the divine majesty under a veil of flesh, and by a most stupendous humiliation indeed come and proclaim peace to a sinful world; from the traditional revelation and expectation of which, till he came, all the fabulous appearances of the heathen deities, however mixed with after-abominations, were derived—and lastly, suffering themselves to be detained on their way by the devout entreaties of these their servants, to shew their ear would ever be open to sincere and fervent prayer, offered in faith; that they would come and dwell by their spirit in every believing heart, that should be found fruitful in good works, of which the particular enjoined by the Apostle in this Scripture is a high and eminent instance; as if he had said— "Remember to be continually doing such kind offices of Christian love, inasmuch as some have, by so doing, entertained even the divine persons themselves, in their œconomical characters;" manifested, as they were wont to be in those days, under such appearances as have been described, to assure the faithful of those times, as well as those that were to come after, that they would always be spiritually present, as I have said, with their Church, dwell in every heart, that should be continually prepared through faith working by love for their reception.

And if this exposition of the above Scripture be admitted, the only remaining objection I can think of to what has been said is the account generally given of this appearance, not only by later expositors, but by most, though not by all of the holy fathers themselves, viz., that one of the persons here spoken of was Jehovah, or God the Son, the other two mere angels, his attendants only ; so that when one person is addressed or speaketh, the divine WORD himself is meant—when the three, the divine WORD and his attendant angels: from which opinion, supported by such high authorities, I should with great diffidence have receded, especially as the Scripture, in the way they understand it, clearly establisheth the divinity of Christ, but that the context evidently requireth a different interpretation. For after Jehovah is said to appear, and the manner of his appearance is described, which is, in three men—" Jehovah appeared unto him, and he lift up his eyes and looked, and lo ! three men stood by him"—there is no mark of inferiority or subordination observable throughout the whole chapter. On the contrary, Abraham runneth to meet them, and equally addresseth the three with the singular appellation of my Lord ; Sarah prepareth three measures of meal, one, as it should seem, for each person ; they are equally invoked to partake of the sacrifice, and equally accept of the invitation; which even if the feast had not been sacrificial, as it was, no ministering spirit in heaven would have attempted; much more, as it was sacrificial, would two of the three in this appearance have corrected the patriarch's mistake with some such reverential language as the following—" See (thou do it) not (to us) for we are thy fellow-servants—worship God;[1] divine honours are due only to one in this appearance, who created us as well as thee," etc. Besides, that Abraham did not address one of them only, who appeared more eminent than the other two, is plain from the behaviour of Lot in the following chapter; who (after one of the persons here expressly styled Jehovah, which had stayed behind in order to reveal his divine counsel to Abraham, and accept his typical intercession thereupon, as a figure of Christ's, and therefore could not be the second person,[2] as hath been generally supposed, had left communing with him, and was gone to his place) addresseth himself in the same manner to the other two, which are there styled angels—" And two of the angels (so it is in the Hebrew[3]) came

---

[1] Rev. xxii, 9.

[2] The learned Dr. Lightfoot hath been beforehand with me in this remark—" The Son and the Holy Ghost," saith he, "go down to Sodom, but the first Person stayeth with Abraham, and condescendeth to his prayer, as long as he asketh."—Vol. i, p. 13.

[3] שני המלאנים—as שני הנשיאים, Numb. vii, 3, is two of the princes, and so rendered by our translators.

to Sodom at even (*i.e.*, two of those which had appeared unto Abraham[1]—so here the three are styled angels), and Lot rose up to meet them, and he bowed himself with his face towards the ground, and he said, Behold now my Lord;"[2] for so it is again in the original, and would have been so in our translation, if the translators had been consistent with themselves, and rendered אדני, not my *Lords*, but my *Lord*, as they have rightly done in the preceding chapter. To which may be subjoined the like variations of the singular and plural numbers, as in the chapter above, as may be seen by comparison; but very remarkably from the twelfth to the twenty-fifth verse, where we read, "That the men said unto Lot, we will destroy this place, because the cry of them is waxen great before Jehovah, and Jehovah hath sent us to destroy it—then the angels hastened Lot—and while he lingered, the men laid hold upon his hand, etc. And it came to pass, when they had brought them forth abroad, that he said, escape for thy life—haste thee, escape thither (to Zoar), for I cannot do anything till thou be come thither.—Then Jehovah rained upon Sodom and upon Gomorrah brimstone and fire from Jehovah out of heaven. Above you see, Lot

---

[1] "The Son and the Holy Ghost," saith Dr. Lightfoot, "come into Sodom to destroy it, and now they are called angels, because they were sent by the Father."—Vol. i, p. 695. See also p. i of the preface to this sermon.

[2] Gen. xix, 1, 2.

called the two angels or men "my Lord;" here, they say, "We will destroy this place—Jehovah hath sent us to destroy it;" and yet a little after, "I cannot do anything till thou be come thither.—Then Jehovah rained," etc. The two therefore, however distinct in personality and offices, were of one nature, the two angels were Jehovah, as well as the person that sent them; which proves a Trinity of persons in the divine nature to a demonstration, each of whom is by plain deduction styled in this Scripture Jehovah, but two apparently and past all contradiction in the twenty-fourth verse—"Jehovah rained upon Sodom, etc.," Jehovah from Jehovah, *i.e.*, the second person, in his œconomical or covenant-office, as judge of the world, from the first.

I will only add a short inference from what has been said, and then, the leading and principal circumstance of the history being thus laid open at large, briefly shew the use we should make of this and the other circumstances thereof, in the practical application of them to ourselves. The inference is this—if the patriarch Abraham believed (as he most certainly did) the doctrine of the ever-blessed Trinity, then was the doctrine of the ever-blessed Trinity an article of faith in the days of Abraham. Indeed, if there was any occasion, and this is a proper place for such an inquiry, I could easily prove this doctrine to have been revealed to our first parents before the fall,[1] and that their hope and

---

[1] The usual word for God, אלהים, is incontestably

comfort, after their transgression, as well as those of all their children since, immediately depended, and must always depend, upon the truth and certainty of it; so that it was then, and ever will be necessary, that all believers should be acquainted with it.

III. And now to proceed to the other circumstances of the history, and the practical application of the whole to ourselves, without which we should omit the great end for which this and every Scripture history was recorded. For very narrow and unworthy conceptions must he have of the manifold wisdom of God, as contrary to the plain declaration of the Scriptures of the New Testament, as derogatory from the spirit of prophecy in the Old, who can think the foregoing, or any other patriarchal history, was designed to terminate in the patriarch himself. This is the case with human histories indeed, but by no means with the divine. "Known unto God are all his works from the beginning of the world"[1]—and in all the works of God from the beginning of the world all the children of God are

---

plural, denoting a plurality of persons in the divine nature, whom other Scriptures determine to be three. If Eve had not understood the word, the tempter would scarce have used it; and unless they had both referred it to the divine persons, on whom Eve was dependent as their creature, I cannot see the force of the temptation—" Ye shall be as Gods"—the Heb. is as אלהים, *i.e.*, grammatically like more divine persons than one, whatever be the radical idea of the word, which is not before me now.

[1] Acts xv, 18.

interested. The lives, actions, etc., of the holy patriarchs, besides their respect to Christ and his spiritual kingdom, are so many lively figures of the spiritual state of every particular Christian, who is a stranger and a sojourner, in this world, as all his fathers were.[1] They had the same faith in the things not seen, the same hope in the world to come; and the same love, springing out of both, was their perfection as well as ours. The things recorded of them were therefore ensamples to us; and of those here recorded of Abraham and Sarah, doubtless for our imitation and encouragement, the following particulars seem most to deserve our attention.

1. No sooner did Jehovah appear unto Abraham, than he ran to meet him. The appearance, I suppose, was a glorious one, miraculously supported in the air, not close-by, but, as the word may well be understood to signify, at some little distance above or over the place where Abraham was sitting; which I only mention to obviate any exception that may be taken at the patriarch's running to meet him. But why did he run to meet him? If thine own heart cannot answer, ask the devout soul and it shall tell thee. Though Jehovah was so nigh unto him, he ran to meet him. Oh! a sense of the divine presence is a wonderful incitement to devotion. And by what outward act could Abraham so

---

[1] Ps. xxxix, 12; Heb. xi, 13; 1 Pet. ii, 11.

well express the inward affection of his soul? As his low prostration of the body on the dust shewed his humility in the sight of God, so did the running of his feet to meet him the very fervent desire of his filial love, his exceeding earnestness to converse with God, and run the way of his commandments.[1] Jehovah appeared—he lifted up his eyes, and looked —and saw—and ran to meet him. And oh! that we, like the father of the faithful, whenever God is pleased to visit us with his grace, would, without a moment's hesitation, run to meet him in the way of his ordinances! Would make haste, and delay not the time to entertain God in our hearts! that our affections, like Abraham's, would ever obey the very first touch of the divine attraction! that we could every one of us address him at such times in his own inimitable language—" Draw me, we will run after thee!"[2]

2. Abraham not only ran to meet God, but prepared with the same alacrity for his reception. He hastened back into the tent—bade Sarah make ready quickly three measures of fine meal for the sacred cakes—he himself ran to the herd for the sacrifice—and his young man hasted to dress it. How expressive all this of the active spirit of true Christian faith! Let us be careful to improve every circumstance to the blessed purposes for which it was written. As holy Sarah, at her lord's command,

---

[1] Ps. cxix, 32.   [2] Song of Solomon, i, 4.

made the sacrificial cakes ready quickly, so let the Church, at her Lord's command, have ever in readiness the bread of life. As Sarah cheerfully obeyed Abraham in this matter with all dutiful subjection, in like manner let the Church be subject to Christ, her head, in all things; taking all her instruction from the blessed word both in points of doctrine and institution, not wise in her own conceit, but opening her ear to heavenly wisdom, doing her Lord's will, not her own, even as he "came down from heaven, not to do (his) own will, but the will of him that sent (him)."[1] "Hearken, O daughter, and consider, and incline thine ear, forget also thine own people, and thy father's house; so shall the king have pleasure in thy beauty, for he (is) thy Lord, and worship thou him."[2] As the young man hasted to dress the sacrifice, let the Levites or deacons, the Lord's ministers, shew the same diligence, in due subordination assisting their superiors, not with eye-service, but from the heart; that they who have appointed them to this ministry may rejoice with them in their pious labours, and they themselves, when the chief Shepherd shall appear, receive the blessed reward of them. As Abraham hastened into his tent, to direct the immediate preparation of the holy cakes—ran to the herd to fetch the sacrifice for his divine guests—and, as soon as the whole was ready, devoutly set it before them

---

[1] John vi, 38.   [2] Ps. xlv, 10, 11.

—so let the bishops and priests, called to be intercessors on earth (who stand in Christ's stead, by his appointment, here between Jehovah and his people), be continually mindful to set before him, for his remembrance, the consecrated signs of his body and blood, the sweet and most comfortable memorials of his meritorious sufferings and our heavenly support, his pledges to us and our claim from him of life everlasting; that so, whenever he shall be pleased to visit us, he may, together with the observance of his other holy ordinances, find us thus doing; and being therefore (for this reason) come to us his servants, as he did of old to his servant Abraham, detained by our fervent devotion and sincere obedience, may not pass away from us, but, according to his most true promise, fulfilled in all believers by the œconomical office of the Holy Comforter after his departure, may come and dwell with us in the tent or tabernacle of his Church in grace, till he taketh us up into his glory—as he said: "If a man love me, he will keep my words; and my Father will love him, and we will come unto him, and make our abode with him."[1] And again, after his ascension: "Behold I stand at the door, and knock: if any man hear my voice, and open the door, I will come in to him and sup with him, and he with me."[2]

3. Consider Abraham's sacrifice—it was the best

---

[1] John xiv, 23.   [2] Rev. iii, 20.

of the kind—the calf he ran to the herd to fetch was tender and good; in which the patriarch not only punctually observed the traditional law, which suffered not the immaculate Son of God to be represented by a creature in any respect imperfect, but moreover, as I doubt not from overflowing gratitude, worshipped God with the best of everything, of things appointed, that he had. In both particulars let us imitate him, in his faith and in his love. Let us believe and trust in the spotless innocence and perfect oblation of our Lord Jesus Christ; and let every spiritual sacrifice and gift we offer through his merits be the most excellent we have. Let us dedicate to God and his glory the first and best of our faculties. Let our early and most unforced meditation, when solitude shall incline the heart to thoughtfulness, be of him; with him let us employ the first hour of every day, especially where the blessed opportunity is afforded us, in his more immediate presence, in his holy temple; and let our hearts at every such time dwell on the riches of his mercy. On him, and the treasure laid up in heaven for us, let us fix our first and best love; and, above all, employ the best season of life in his word and in his service—" Remember now thy creators,"[1] the persons who have created thee out of nothing, and have since, if thou art a Christian, created thy soul again, as they will thy body at the resurrection of

---

[1] בּוֹרְאֶיךָ, plural.

the dead, after the image of Christ, remember these divine persons in the day of thy youth.

4. Faithful Sarah first doubted, afterwards believed, and obtained the promise. The Church militant, like its emblem in the material heavens, hath its waxes and wanings, and there is no believer on the earth but hath experienced both. For our encouragement under occasional infirmities this circumstance of Sarah therefore seemeth to be written; and it containeth large matter for consolation, though not the least for presumption. Sarah's doubts were not of the infidel kind—no, she was sincere in the faith; but the suddenness and greatness of the promise overpowered her faith, till the consideration of God's almighty power (is anything too hard for Jehovah?) re-established it. Thus it may happen to the best of Christians, only let us guard against wilful ignorance; and then a true and genuine faith in God will be consistent with our infirmities. Let us be careful, after every such surprise, to follow Sarah in her faith, that so we may be found of that happy number who were to partake of her joy; that finally apprehending all the promises of God in Christ, and stedfastly believing the things we have " not seen, we may rejoice here with joy unspeakable and full of glory,"[1] and hereafter be received up into that glory, to see all we have be-

---

[1] 1 Pet. i, 8.

lieved here—"For blessed (are) they that have not seen and (yet) have believed."¹

5. Lastly, Abraham when he received the promise was celebrating the ordinances of God; and shall any that name the name of Christ, now the promise is accomplished, presume to neglect and despise them? "Unto us a child is born, unto us a son is given,"² even "the promised seed"³ of whose incarnation the birth of Isaac was only a figure, the shadow of whose day Abraham saw,⁴ and in the brightness of whose day we live.⁵ And shall any called by his holy name, I repeat it through astonishment, as well as for enforcement, shall any, called Christians, contemn the institutions of God, under pretence of a more spiritual and refined mode of worship? Was the Church of Christ, from the promise to Adam, ever without external emblems or sacraments? Abraham, the friend of God, received not God out of the way of his ordinances: let us herein discern the only acceptable way of gaining the friendship of God. The outward ordinances of God's appointment are of the same importance now as then. The mere ordinances indeed, without the spirit of religion, will not profit to salvation; but no more will faith of itself without the use of the appointed means, the rejection of which, in any respect, is as

---

¹ John xx, 29.   ² Is. ix, 6.
³ Gen. iii, 15; xxii, 17, 18; Ps. lxxxix, 4; Gal. iii, 16.
⁴ John viii, 56.   ⁵ 1 John ii, 8.

profane as it is unreasonable. This did not Abraham—he had faith, and sacrificed. His faith in Christ superseded not the necessity of showing his death till he came in the flesh; nor will our's that of showing the same till he come in his glory—" For as often as ye eat this bread, and drink this cup, ye do shew the Lord's death till he come."[1]

To conclude, and I mention it last that it may leave a deep impression upon your minds, follow Abraham then in his faith, that ye may be " the children of the promise."[2] " Abraham," saith the Apostle to the Galatians, " believed God, and it was imputed to him for righteousness. Know ye therefore, and they which are of faith, the same are the children of Abraham. For the Scripture, foreseeing that God would justify the heathen through faith, preached before (*i.e.*, before the law) the gospel to Abraham, (saying) in thy seed (which is Christ) shall all the gentiles be blessed—so then they which be of the faith are blessed with faithful Abraham."[3] " Our forefather Abraham therefore" (we may say with St. Cyril) "was not ignorant, that the maker of heaven and earth and all that is therein, who had power over all things, was worshipped in a Holy Trinity; nor were those that sprang from him, viz., Isaac and Jacob, of a different opinion: but treading in the steps of their father's virtue,

---

[1] 1 Cor. xi, 26.   [2] Rom. ix, 8.   [3] Gal. iii, 9.

became likewise zealous assertors of his faith."[1] And oh! that the present age followed them, as they did their father Abraham; did not—under the clear light of the gospel-day they so much desired to see, to the disgrace of many once noble and illustrious families amongst us—basely degenerate from both! But do you, my brethren, by prayer and diligent reading of God's holy word, endeavour all of you after his faith, that ye may be blessed with him. He believed the doctrine I am enforcing in the fullest manner: whoever believeth it not, is no spiritual son of Abraham, hath no title to grace here, or to glory hereafter. Let no man therefore beguile you of your everlasting inheritance, the only foundation of which is faith in the ever-blessed Trinity in Unity. For if there be not three persons in the Godhead, there is no Redeemer; who then hath fulfilled the law for you, and paid the atonement for your sins, since he who was able to do this must be God as well as man, and if this is not done ye are yet in your sins? If there be not three persons in the Godhead there is no Holy Spirit; who can then "create in you a clean heart, and renew a right spirit within you," since a spiritual creation is as much a work of divine incommunicable power as a natural one? Who then shall sanctify and support you, who conduct you on your way? Whence you may observe, this doctrine of the holy Trinity is not an

---

[1] St. Cyril. Alex. contr. Julian. Lib. i, p. 21.

article of mere speculation, as some, that have no interest in it, assert. No—it is the very basis and essence, you see, of the Christian religion, inseparably interwoven and indissolubly connected with every doctrine and precept of it; which (taking in the patriarchal and legal dispensations of it) is, exclusive of all other religions in the world, the religion of the Trinity, being wholly made up of the several parts each divine person undertook, and either hath already fulfilled, or will most assuredly fulfil, for the restoration of man; and which, without this leading doctrine of a co-equal co-eternal personalty in the divine nature, upon the truth and certainty of which the Christian covenant and execution thereof by consequence depend, whatever encomiums may be bestowed on its moral duties, when abstracted from this their only root and foundation, (all, I fear, intended, like the kiss Judas gave their author, to spoil them of their life) must, like every after scheme of diabolic and human contrivance that beareth the name of religion, leave the polluted offspring of fallen Adam still weltering in their blood[1]—rebels, under the original attainder—insolvent debtors, in the infernal prison—sinners, in the hand of a just God, unransomed and unforgiven—hard-hearted, impenitent, unchanged, bewildered, comfortless, and accursed. But if you believe this doctrine with a sincere heart, keeping his command-

---

[1] Ezek. xvi, 6.

ments who hath loved you, you may look up with confidence to the persons who have covenanted to save you, "who will never leave you nor forsake you,"[1] but will accomplish your salvation. Let the blind infidel, the man of this world, who walketh on in spiritual darkness, "loving that darkness still rather than light, because his deeds are evil,"[2] let such, lost as they are to God and dead to every thing that is good, reject, to their own destruction, this adorable doctrine—blaspheme the holy truths they cannot in that state apprehend[3]—and despise the hope and joy an unconverted heart never felt or can experience ; but let it be your glory, my brethren, always, as it will ever be your happiness, publicly to confess before men and angels, the ever-blessed Trinity in Unity—the God of all believers since the world began—the God of Abraham, Isaac, and Jacob—the God of Israel, and our God, the God and Father of our Lord Jesus Christ.

Unto whom be glory in the Church by Christ Jesus, throughout all ages, world without end. Amen.

---

[1] Josh. i, 5 ; Heb. xiii, 5.   [2] John iii, 19.
[3] 1 Cor. ii, xiv.

LIST OF SUBSCRIBERS.

A.
The Lord Auckland, Bishop of Bath and Wells
Atherton, Miss Eleanora, Kersall Cell, near Manchester (3 copies)
Allcroft, Jeremiah, Esq., Lower Wick, Worcestershire

B.
Bruce, the Right Hon. the Lord Justice (2 copies)
Bulley, the Rev. Dr., President of Magdalen College, Oxford
Bright, the Rev. Wm., Fellow of ditto
Braikenridge, Rev. G. W., M.A., formerly Member of University College, Clevedon, Somerset
Barwis, Mrs., Chipping Norton, Oxon. (4 copies)

C.
Coleridge, the Right Hon. Sir J. T., Heath's Court, Ottery St. Mary, Devon
Churton, the Rev. Edward, Archdeacon of Cleveland, Yorkshire (2 copies)
Claughton, the Rev. T. L., M.A., Vicar of Kidderminster
Crowther, Rev. William, M.A., Incumbent of Claines, Worcestershire
Curtler, Rev. T. G., M.A., Aclaston, Norfolk (2 copies)
Curtler, T. G., Esq., Bevere House, Claines, Worcestershire
Curtler, Martin, Esq.
Carlyon, Clement D. M., Truro, Cornwall
Clarke, John Graham, Esq., Frocester, Gloucestershire
Carden, H. D., Esq., Worcester
Cooke, Matthew, Esq., George Street, London
Child, Mr. Richard, Worcester
Coombes, Mr. James, Bookseller, Worcester

D.
Darell, the Rev. Sir William Lionel, M.A., Bart. Rector of Fretherne, Gloucestershire
Douglas, Rev. W. W., M.A., Salwarpe Rectory, Worcestershire
Dixon, Mrs., Abbey House, Carlisle (4 copies)
Druitt, Miss, Wimborne Minster (2 copies)
Dent, J. C., Esq., Sudeley Castle, Gloucestershire (2 copies)
Deighton and Son, Messrs., Booksellers, Worcester

E.

Ellacombe, Rev. H. T., M.A., Rectory, Clyst St. George, Devon
Elton, Sir Arthur Hallam, Bart., Clevedon, Somersetshire (2 copies)
Eaton, Mr. Daniel, Bookseller, Worcester

F.

Fraser, James Wilson, Esq., Ingleborough, Settle, Yorkshire

G.

Gladstone, the Right Hon. William Ewart, Chancellor of the Exchequer, Downing Street, Westminster
Godfery, the Rev. W., M.A., Rectory, Martin Hussingtree, Worcestershire (2 copies)
Gibson, Rev. John, M.A., Rectory, King's Stanley, Gloucestershire
Gutch, George, Esq., Porteus House, Paddington (2 copies)
Gutch, John James, Esq., York
Gutch, J. W. G., Esq., Charlotte Street, London
Gutch, Mrs. Robert, Norton St. Philip, Bath
Gutch, Miss, Oxford (2 copies)
Gutch, Miss Sarah (2 copies)
Grainger, Mr. Thomas, Bookseller, Worcester

H.

Hamilton, the Very Rev. H. P., F.R.S., Dean of Salisbury, Deanery
Havergal, Rev. W. H., M.A., Shareshill, Wolverhampton (2 copies)
Hodson, Rev. George, M.A., Rector of All Saints, Worcester
Hooper, Rev. J. B., M.A., Rectory, Upton Warren
Holmes, Rev. George G., M.A., King's Stanley
Hope, Alexander J. Beresford, Esq., D.C.L., Arklow House, Connaught Place, London
Hill, Matthew Devonport, Esq., Commissioner of Bankruptcy, Bristol
Hooper, A. C., Esq., Worcester

J.

Johnson, Rev. J. G., M.A., Worcester
Jones, Rev. Thomas, M.A., Worcester

K.

Kilvert, Rev. Francis, M.A., Claverton Lodge, Bath

King, Miss, Frocester, Gloucestershire (2 copies)

L.

Lyttelton, the Right Honourable Lord, Lord Lieutenant of Worcestershire, Hagley Park
Lygon, the Honourable Frederick, M.P., Madresfield Court, Worcester
Lechmere, Sir Edmund, Bart., The Rhydd, Worcestershire
Lechmere, Rev. A. B., Vicar and Rural Dean of Hanley, ditto
Lea, John Wheeley, Esq., Stanfield House, near Worcester
Lavender, Miss, Barbourne, Worcester (2 copies)

M.

Medd, Rev. P. G., Fellow of University College
Massingberd, Rev. F. C., M.A., Ormsby, near Alford, Lincolnshire
Moor, the Rev. John Frewen, M.A., Bath
Markland, J. H., Esq., D.C.L., Bath (2 copies)

N.

Nichols, John Bowyer, Esq., F.S.A., Parliament St., London
Nichols, John Gough, Esq., F.S.A.,   ditto

O.

Oldham, Rev. James, M.A., Rectory, Dover Dale, Worcestershire
Oldham, Thomas, Esq., Bevere, Worcestershire

P.

Peel, the Very Rev. John, D.D., Dean of Worcester, Deanery (3 copies)
Plumptre, the Rev. J. G., Master of University College (5 copies)
Prevost, the Rev. Sir G., Bart., Rural Dean, Winchcomb, Dursley
Parker, the Rev. William, M.A., Rectory, Great Comberton, Worcestershire (2 copies)
Philpott, Rev. Thomas, M.A., Belbroughton, Worcestershire
Popham, Rev. John, M.A., Rector of St. Andrew, Droitwich, Worcestershire
Palmer, Rev. John, M.A., Vicar of Bromyard, Herefordshire
Palmer, Roundell, Esq., Queen's Counsel, London
Pakington, the Right Hon. Sir John, Bart., Westwood Park, Worcestershire

Pinder, Rev. Canon, M.A., Principal of the Theological College, Wells

R.
Rennick, Walker, Esq., Worcester
Refton, F. B., Esq., Dacre Park, Greenwich (3 copies)

S.
Shipton, the Rev. J. N., D.D., Vicarage, Othery, Bridgewater, Somerset
Spooner, Richard, Esq., M.P., Birmingham
Shirley, Evelyn Philip, Esq., M.P., Eatington Park, Warwickshire
Sidebottom, Charles, Esq., Worcester
Stallard, Josiah, Esq., Worcester
Stratford, Mr., Bookseller, Worcester

T.
Thorn, Rev. William, M.A., Thames House, Worcester, formerly of University College
Tymbs, H. B., Esq., Worcester

U. and V.
University College Library, Oxford
Viner, Rev. Alfred Ellis, Vicar of Badgworth, Gloucestershire, formerly of University College

W.
Worcester, the Right Rev. the Lord Bishop of, Hartlebury Castle
Wood, Rev. John Ryle, M.A., Canon of Worcester
Wordsworth, Rev. Canon, Cloisters, Westminster
Wilson, Rev. J., D.D., President of Trinity College, Oxford
Wood, Sir Wm. Page, Vice-Chancellor
Winnington, Sir Thos., Bart., M.P., Stanford Court, Worcestershire (2 copies)
Walker, Rev. Thomas, M.A., Rectory, Abbot Morton, Worcestershire
Walker, G. J. A., Esq., Norton Villa, Whittington, Worcestershire
Wort, Rev. William, M.A., Curate of Hawarden, Flintshire

Y.
Yapp, Richard, Esq., Halesend, Great Malvern

www.ingramcontent.com/pod-product-compliance
Lightning Source LLC
Chambersburg PA
CBHW020830230426
43666CB00007B/1167